The New Scarlet Letter:

The New Scarlet Letter?

Negotiating the U.S. Labor Market with a Criminal Record

Steven Raphael

2014

W.E. Upjohn Institute for Employment Research
Kalamazoo, Michigan

Library of Congress Cataloging-in-Publication Data

Raphael, Steven, 1968-
    The new scarlet letter? : negotiating the U.S. labor market with a criminal record /
Steven Raphael.
        pages cm. — (We focus)
    Includes bibliographical references and index.
    ISBN 978-0-88099-479-8 (pbk. : alk. paper) — ISBN 0-88099-479-7 (pbk. : alk.
paper)
    1. Ex-convicts—Employment—United States. 2. Criminals—Rehabilitation—
United States. 3. Labor market—United States. I. Title.
    HV9304.R36 2014
    331.5'10973—dc23
                                2014014740

© 2014
W.E. Upjohn Institute for Employment Research
300 S. Westnedge Avenue
Kalamazoo, Michigan 49007-4686

Cover design by Alcorn Publication Design.
Index prepared by Diane Worden.
Printed in the United States of America.
Printed on recycled paper.

For Kelly, Antonio, and Ariana,
my endless sources of love and inspiration.

Contents

1 **Mass Incarceration and Employment**   1
The Scale and Scope of Incarceration in the United States   3
Outline of the Book   10

2 **Why Are So Many Americans in Prison?**   13
The Determinants of a Country's Incarceration Rate   16
Specific Policy Changes Driving Incarceration Growth   21
Implications for the Employment of Former Prisoners   24

3 **A Portrait of Future, Current, and Former Prison Inmates**   27
Future Prison Inmates   28
Current Prison Inmates   34
Former Prison Inmates   38
Implications for the Employment of Former Prisoners   41

4 **Employers' Perceptions of Former Inmates**   43
What Do Employers Think about Ex-Offenders?   44
How Do Employers Find Out About an Applicant's Criminal   47
History Record?
Hiring Outcomes and Employment Prospects   52
Implications for the U.S. Labor Market   56

5 **Employment-Based Prisoner Reentry Programs: Do We Know**   59
What Works?
Experimental versus Nonexperimental Evaluations of Prisoner   61
Reentry Programs
Results from Experimental Evaluations of Employment-Based   64
Programs
Implications for the Employment of Former Prisoners   75

6 **Policies for Moving Forward**   79
Scaling Back the Use of Incarceration as Punishment   81
Improving the Process of Triaging the Reentry Population   84
Sharing the Risk with Employers   88

References   91

Author   97

Index   99

About the Institute   107

Figures

1.1   Percentage of U.S. Adult Men Ever Incarcerated in a State or Federal   7
       Prison and the Lifetime Likelihood of Going to Prison for a Male
       Child Born in 2001
1.2   Percentage of U.S. Adult Women Ever Incarcerated in a State or Federal   8
       Prison and the Lifetime Likelihood of Going to Prison for a Female
       Child Born in 2001

2.1   Incarceration Rates in the United States and Other Countries   14
       (Various Years, 2008–2011)
2.2   Number of State and Federal Prisoners per 100,000 U.S. Residents,   15
       1925–2011
2.3   Admissions to Prison per 100,000 U.S. Residents by Offense Type,   17
       1984 and 2009
2.4   Crime Rates, Arrests per Crime, and Prison Admissions per Arrest in   19
       2009 Relative to 1984 by Offense Type
2.5   Time Served, by Offense, 1984 and 2009   20

3.1   Distribution of Total Years of Work Experience among Female NLSY97   33
       Respondents by the 2010 Interview
3.2   Distribution of Total Years of Work Experience among Male NLSY97   34
       Respondents by the 2010 Interview

4.1   How Willing Would You Be to Accept an Applicant with Various   45
       Characteristics? A California Employer Responds

Tables

1.1   Percentage of Adults Aged 18–65 Incarcerated in 2007, by Gender and   5
       Race/Ethnicity

3.1   Demographic Characteristics of Youth in 1997 Who Are Eventually   29
       Incarcerated by 2010 and Youth Who Are Not
3.2   Academic Performance, Eventual Educational Attainment, and   31
       Self-Reported Delinquent Behavior in 1997 of Youth Who Are
       Eventually Incarcerated by 2010 and Youth Who Are Not (%)
3.3   Characteristics of State and Federal Prisoners in 2004   36
3.4   Characteristics of Prisoners Released from State Prison in 2003   39

Chapter 1

Mass Incarceration
and Employment

In 2011, nearly 700,000 people were released from either a state or federal prison. These releases added to the roughly six million adults who have served prison time in the past. Many will experience a host of difficulties upon reentering noninstitutional society. Those with minor children (especially incarcerated men) often accumulate substantial back child-support obligations while incarcerated and face the legal requirement to pay down the balance. Many face precarious housing situations and a high risk of homelessness following release. Most have little in the way of assets and receive a very small amount of "gate money" upon release, usually no more than a few hundred dollars. Many will be returned to custody for either parole violations or a new felony offense. In light of these problems and the sheer number of individuals released from our prisons each year, policymakers at all levels of government are increasingly focused on how to foster and support the successful reentry of former prison inmates.

For a myriad of reasons, stable employment is of central importance to the successful reentry of former inmates into noninstitutionalized society. To start, the material well-being of most released inmates depends principally on what they can earn in the labor market. The U.S. social safety net provides little by way of public assistance for the nonworking poor, especially for able-bodied and nonelderly men. Thus, avoiding material poverty requires gainful employment.

Second, economic research has demonstrated that the likelihood of committing crime depends to some extent on having something to lose. Those with good jobs and good employment prospects in the legitimate labor market tend to commit less crime; those with poor employment prospects tend to commit more. Higher criminal participation among those with low earnings may be driven by the need to generate income to meet basic needs, a sense that the potential losses associated with being caught and punished are low when legitimate job opportunities are rare, or a general sense of not playing a meaningful role outside of prison. Regardless of the causal avenue, the transition to stable employment is often characterized as a key determinant of desistance from criminal activity and the process of disentangling oneself from the criminal justice system.

Third, most released inmates are of an age where most men are firmly attached to the labor force and where conventional norms regarding responsible adult behavior prescribe steady legitimate work and supporting one's dependents. Facilitating "buy in" among former inmates into conventional society requires that they be afforded the opportunity to transition into the standard roles of other law-abiding citizens.

Finally, formal employment provides daily structure and a sense of purpose for many—factors that may prevent further criminal activity. Criminologists have studied in-depth the "incapacitation effect" of prison—that is, the extent to which prisons reduce crime by forcibly segregating the criminally active. Of course, many other activities incapacitate criminal activity, if we interpret the word *incapacitation* broadly. Schools tend to reduce the criminal activity of youth by keeping them busy during the day. Marriage tends to incapacitate the criminal activity of young men as the accompanying newfound responsibilities and activities supplant more crime-prone settings and pursuits. Extending the metaphor to the labor market, having something to do during the day that generates legitimate income leaves less time for committing crime. Moreover, daily exposure to coworkers who are more firmly attached to legitimate work and less involved in crime may provide an alternative set of positive role models demonstrating how to live one's life within the bounds of the law.

Unfortunately, the employment prospects of many former inmates upon leaving prison are bleak. Moreover, most face many challenges specific to former prisoners that are likely to hamper their labor market prospects for years to come. Of paramount importance are the characteristics of former inmates themselves. Those who serve time in prison are far from a representative cross section of the U.S. adult population. Inmates, and former inmates, are disproportionately male, have very low levels of formal educational attainment, are disproportionately minority, have unstable employment histories, and often have a history of substance abuse problems. In addition, the prevalence of severe mental illness is quite high. Independent of having a criminal record, most of these characteristics are predictive of poor employment outcomes in the U.S. labor market in their own right.

These factors are compounded by the general wariness of employers and the stigma associated with a criminal history and having served time in a prison. A consistent finding in surveys of employers is a strong reluctance to hire an applicant with a criminal history, and an increasing tendency of employers to either directly ask an applicant about one's history or to use third-party firms to conduct more formal and thorough background checks.

In this book I explore the labor market prospects of the growing population of former prison inmates in the United States. In particular, I document the specific challenges created by the characteristics of this population and the common hiring and screening practices of U.S. employers. In addition, I discuss various policy efforts to improve the employment prospects and limit the future criminal activity of former prison inmates either through improving the skills and qualifications of these job seekers or through the provision of incentives to employers to hire such individuals.

THE SCALE AND SCOPE OF INCARCERATION IN THE UNITED STATES

Although the United States technically has 51 separate criminal justice systems (one for each state and the federal government), we can divide those incarcerated on any given day into three broad groups: 1) those serving time in a local jail, 2) those serving time in a state prison, and 3) those serving time in a federal prison. County jail inmates are usually those awaiting trial or arraignment, those convicted of misdemeanor and sometimes felony offenses where the sentence to be served is less than one year, and prisoners awaiting transfer to state prison. State prisons hold inmates who have been tried and convicted in state court for violating state law and who are sentenced to at least one year. In recent years, this population increasingly includes drug offenders and inmates who have violated the conditions of their parole, though felony property and violent offenders still make up the substantial majority (roughly two-thirds) of the state inmate population. Federal prisons hold inmates who have violated federal law. In recent years, this population has become overwhelmingly composed of inmates convicted of a select few crimes, with drug felonies (55 percent) and weapons violations (11 percent) making up the lion's share.

There are also two broad groups of individuals residing in the community who are technically still under the supervision of the criminal justice system. Those on probation are usually those convicted of misdemeanors or felonies that are granted a sentence of probation in lieu of a prison or jail term. Probation officers are county employees and coordinate directly with local criminal justice officials from various agencies. Those who violate the terms of their probation may be punished by a spell in prison or jail. Inmates conditionally released from prison are usually supervised in the community by state parole authorities.[1] These releases are often required to meet periodically with their parole officers, must refrain from various activities such as abusing drugs or engaging in further crime, and often are unable to leave their county of residence while on parole. Violating the terms of one's parole can result in a jail spell, a return to prison, or some other form of graduated sanction that does not involve a further incarceration.

As of 2011, there were approximately 2.3 million persons incarcerated in either a state or federal prison or a county jail. Of this total, 1.4 million were in a state prison; 216,000 were in a federal prison; and 736,000 were in a county jail (Carson and Golinelli 2013; Minton 2013). The overwhelming majority of these inmates are eventually released back into society. Among state prisoners, roughly 81 percent in any year expect to leave prison within the next four calendar years, with nearly half expecting to be released within the year. Among federal prisoners, two-thirds expect to be released within four calendar years, and roughly one-quarter expect to be released within the year.

I will postpone a more detailed portrait of inmates until Chapter 3. To start the conversation, however, Table 1.1 presents estimates combining data from the Bureau of Justice Statistics (BJS) and the U.S. Census Bureau of the proportion of adults aged 18–65 in 2007 who were incarcerated on any given day. The table displays figures for adults in this age range by gender and by broad racial/ethnic groups

Table 1.1 Percentage of Adults Aged 18–65 Incarcerated in 2007, by Gender and Race/Ethnicity

	Incarcerated in any institution	Incarcerated in a county jail	Incarcerated in a state prison	Incarcerated in a federal prison
All men	2.2	0.7	1.3	0.2
Non-Hispanic white	1.1	0.4	0.8	0.1
Non-Hispanic black	7.9	2.5	4.7	0.8
Hispanic	2.7	0.9	1.5	0.3
Non-Hispanic other	1.1	0.3	0.6	0.1
All women	0.2	0.1	0.1	0.0
Non-Hispanic white	0.1	0.1	0.1	0.0
Non-Hispanic black	0.6	0.3	0.3	0.0
Hispanic	0.2	0.1	0.1	0.0
Non-Hispanic other	0.1	0.0	0.0	0.0

NOTE: Totals are not exact because of rounding.
SOURCE: Raphael and Stoll (2013).

to highlight some of the key disparities. Slightly more than 2 percent of men are incarcerated on any given day, with roughly 80 percent of these men in a state or federal prison. The percentage of women incarcerated is much smaller by comparison (0.2 percent). Table 1.1 also reveals enormous racial and ethnic disparities in the percent incarcerated, with the percentage of black males in prison or jail on any given day more than seven times the figure for white males, and the percentage for Hispanic males roughly two and a half times that of white males. The ordering of the racial differential among women is similar, though the disparities are muted relative to what we see among men.

Perhaps a more relevant way to characterize the scope of incarceration for the purposes of understanding the consequences for the U.S. labor market is to discuss the proportion of individuals who at some point in their lives have served time or will serve time in prison. Such a characterization would help us understand the extent and dimensions of the subpopulation of U.S. adults that have been physically removed from the workforce and that now have a prison spell on record for the remainder of their work careers. Fortunately, the BJS has produced such figures for broad categories of U.S. adults, while independent researchers have produced estimates for specific subgroups of interest.

Figure 1.1 presents BJS estimates of the proportion of adult men in the United States who have served time in a state or federal prison in 2001, as well as the projected chance that a male child born in 2001 will serve prison time at some point in their lives. Naturally, both estimates are much larger than the percentage of men incarcerated on any given day. For example, 2.6 percent of white men have served prison time at some point in their lives, while the figures in Table 1.1 indicate that on any given day only 0.9 percent of white men are in prison. Over 16 percent of African American men have served time in prison, while 5.5 percent are incarcerated on any given day.

The BJS estimates of the lifetime chances of serving prison time are truly staggering. They indicate that fully one-third of African American male children born in 2001 can expect to serve time in

Figure 1.1 Percentage of U.S. Adult Men Ever Incarcerated in a State or Federal Prison and the Lifetime Likelihood of Going to Prison for a Male Child Born in 2001

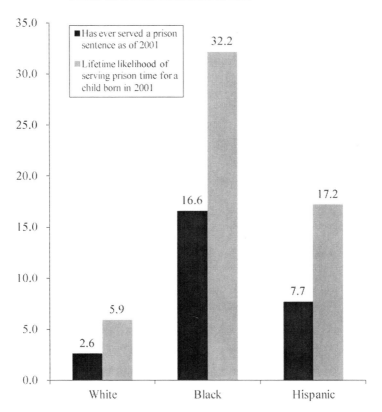

SOURCE: Bonczar (2003).

prison at some point in their lives. The comparable figures for Hispanics and whites are 17.2 and 5.9 percent, respectively.

Figure 1.2 presents comparable results for women. Again, we see much lower rates for women relative to men, yet higher percentages ever serving time than are incarcerated in prisons on any given day. Black women are by far the most likely to have done time and face

Figure 1.2 Percentage of U.S. Adult Women Ever Incarcerated in a State or Federal Prison and the Lifetime Likelihood of Going to Prison for a Female Child Born in 2001

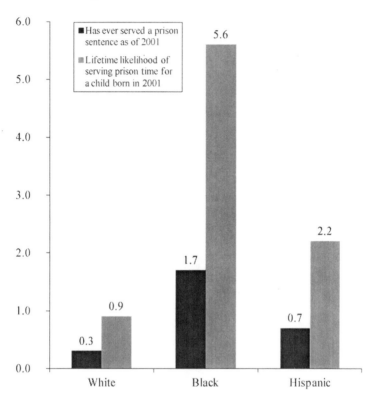

SOURCE: Bonczar (2003).

the highest chances of a prison spell at some point in their lives. The absolute disparities between women of different race and ethnicity, however, are much smaller than what we observe among men.

To be sure, these estimates mask enormous differences that exist when we split the population along various additional dimensions. For example, in Chapter 2 we will document the explosive growth in the nation's overall incarceration rate that began during the mid-

1970s. The growing incarceration rate coupled with the documented fact that people are most criminally active during their teens and early twenties means that younger generations in the United States coming of age during the prison boom face much higher risks of serving prison time than older generations.

Sociologists Becky Pettit and Bruce Western estimate that roughly one-fifth of black men born between 1965 and 1969 served prison time by 1999, a figure roughly four percentage points higher than the figure for black men overall (Pettit and Western 2004). As this birth cohort was roughly 30–34 years of age in 1999 and younger on average than the average adult black male in this year, this fact implies that the prevalence of a past prison spell is higher among younger African American males compared to older African American males.

Moreover, there are enormous disparities in educational attainment among the proportion that have ever been to prison. High school dropouts are the most likely to have done time, with male high school dropouts, particularly black male high school dropouts, having a particularly high incidence of prior prison incarcerations. For the birth cohort that Pettit and Western (2004) study, the authors find that nearly 60 percent of black male high school dropouts served prison time by their early thirties. In some of my own research on California, I found that nearly 90 percent of the state's black male high school dropouts had served prison time by the end of the 1990s (Raphael 2006).

On any given day, a small minority of the adult population is incarcerated in the nation's prisons and jails. However, the population that has ever served time or that will serve time is considerably larger. The large racial disparities and the disparities in incarceration rates by educational attainment that we have briefly touched upon suggests that the particular handicap of a prior prison record disproportionately impacts those who are already at a disadvantage in the U.S. labor market. Hence, the incidence of criminal justice involvement in the United States may be aggravating already existing inequities.

OUTLINE OF THE BOOK

The connections between the rise of mass incarceration and the U.S. labor market are numerous and complex. Greater proportions of the workforce passing through prisons at some point in time may lower formal work experience and worsen the soft and hard skills of those who are incarcerated. Prior incarceration creates a new widespread source of stigma that increasingly affects groups that traditionally underperform in the labor market. Employers who rely heavily on low-skilled workers face new issues and potential liabilities regarding how to take into account criminal history records in hiring decisions. Moreover, policymakers at the local, state, and federal levels are becoming increasingly involved in regulating the labor market for former offenders.

This book will analytically approach the labor market for former prison inmates by sequentially studying the factors that influence the market's supply and demand sides. In Chapter 2, I provide an overview of the forces that have led to the unusually high U.S. incarceration rate and, in turn, an increase in the supply of former prison inmates. Since most prison inmates are eventually released after a relatively short spell in prison, the growth in the U.S. incarceration rate over the past three decades has generated a large supply of former prison inmates. In theory, rising crime rates, tougher sentencing, or some combination of the two may all contribute to increased incarceration rates. In Chapter 2, I show that nearly all of the growth in the U.S. incarceration rate is driven by policy changes at the state and federal levels that have increased the likelihood that a convicted offender is sent to prison, as well as increased the amount of time that someone sent to prison can expect to serve. The main policy changes responsible for this trend are a shift toward determinate sentencing, a series of sentencing reforms ushered into practice via the War on Drugs, and legislation increasing the number and severity of mandatory minimum sentences at both the state and federal levels.

Chapter 3 presents an empirical portrait of the prison population, of recently released prisoners, and of youth who eventually are sent to prison as young adults. The portrait is sobering. Those who serve time are overwhelmingly male, disproportionately minority, and have very low levels of formal education. The prevalence of both substance abuse problems and severe mental illness is quite high. Youth who eventually do time exhibit early delinquency and do poorly in school. Many of these characteristics are already predictive of low earnings and weak labor force attachment. However, it should be noted that in decades past, many of these men would not have served prison time and exhibited high rates of labor force participation. In general, the chapter paints a portrait of a mostly male population who are more likely than not to have grown up poor, and who would likely fare poorly in the labor market for reasons other than their criminal histories.

Employers tend to express a strong reluctance to hire former prison inmates and those with criminal records. Moreover, employers frequently act on this reluctance by asking applicants about their criminal records, conducting formal criminal background checks, or by simply guessing who is likely to have a criminal record based on observed personal characteristics. In Chapter 4, I review what we know about how employers use criminal histories in screening job applicants. I present a discussion of the information infrastructure in the United States that generates the content of criminal background checks and the recent Equal Employment Opportunity Commission guidance on how such information can lawfully be used. I also discuss empirical research on the effects of a criminal record on labor market outcomes. This research reveals a large causal effect of having a prior incarceration spell on the likelihood of being called back for an interview and poor employment outcomes for those who have done time.

A number of efforts have aimed to improve employment outcomes for former inmates, including work release programs, usually involving inmates who are about to be released; traditional workforce development efforts (basic skills remediation, job search assistance); and programs based on transitional job provision. Many of these efforts have been evaluated using randomized control trials, and many others have fairly high-quality nonexperimental evaluations. In Chapter 5, I review this research and condense the findings to what seems to work.

In Chapter 6, I offer policy recommendations aimed at improving the employment prospects of former inmates and ultimately facilitating reintegration into conventional noninstitutionalized society. A reluctance to hire former inmates stems in part from fear of legal liability should a former inmate harm someone on the employer's watch, as well as concerns about the reliability and honesty of these individuals. These concerns could be addressed by more formal and clear guidance about what is expected of employers in the screening process, and perhaps through public efforts to ensure against employer liability. Moreover, there is great room for workforce intermediaries to screen former prisoners. Recent research on criminal desistance suggests that at least one-third of released inmates completely desist upon walking out of the prison gates. Those who successfully complete workforce training programs (obviously a select group) tend to reoffend at very, very low levels. We should devote more effort to harnessing the signals from such programs and use them to reassure employers about specific applicants.

Note

1. Recent corrections reform in California provides an important exception. In 2011, California altered its community corrections system for released prison inmates so that those inmates convicted of a nonsexual/nonviolent/nonserious crime (referred to as "triple-nons" by corrections policy wonks) are now supervised by local probation departments. Those convicted of more serious crimes are still monitored by state parole officers.

Chapter 2

Why Are So Many
Americans in Prison?

A skeptical reader may wonder why one would want to focus on a prior prison spell as a possible determinant of labor market outcomes in the United States. As I alluded to in Chapter 1, and as I document in greater detail in Chapter 3, current, former, and future inmates are far from a representative sample of American adults. They tend to come from poverty, abuse drugs, and have low levels of formal educational attainment and inconsistent employment histories. Minorities are heavily overrepresented, especially African American males, and may face discrimination in the labor market on this basis alone. Most importantly, some might argue that their documented criminal behavior reveals poor judgment and a general lack of trustworthiness and reliability. In light of these facts, one might argue that we should focus less on the consequences of their involvement with the criminal justice system and more on the underlying characteristics of this population and the way these characteristics are valued (or perhaps more appropriately, not valued) by employers in the legitimate labor market.

There are reasons, however, to question this point of view. First, the United States incarcerates its citizens (most are indeed native born) at a rate that far exceeds every other country in the world and greatly exceeds the rates observed among other high-income nations. Figure 2.1 documents this fact with total incarceration rates (the number of prison and jail inmates combined) for the United States, for 15 original members of the European Union, Canada, Mexico, and for the country with the median incarceration rate (that is, the country for which half the nations have a lower rate and half have a higher rate).[1] The U.S. incarceration rate is much greater than the rates for each European country and quite a bit higher than those for Canada and

Figure 2.1 Incarceration Rates in the United States and Other Countries (Various Years, 2008–2011)

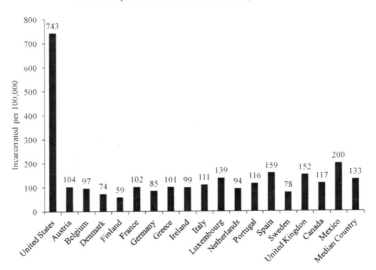

SOURCE: International Centre for Prison Studies (2011).

Mexico. The U.S. rate is over five and half times that of the country with the median rate.

Crime rates in the United States are no higher than they are in Europe, though our violent crime tends to be more lethal because of the proliferation of handguns. However, the percent of prison inmates who are serving time for murder is relatively small (roughly 14 percent) and certainly cannot explain the difference between the United States and, say, the United Kingdom. Assuming that Americans are no more criminally prone than the citizens of European nations, the specifics of the U.S. criminal justice system must somehow be generating these relatively high incarceration rates and, by extension, the large pool of former prisoners.

Second, the U.S. incarceration rate was not always so high. In fact, prior to the mid-1970s, U.S. incarceration rates did not differ appreciably from those in Europe. Figure 2.2 demonstrates this for the prison incarceration rate (the data series for which we have the longest time series). Between 1925 and 1975, the number of prisoners per 100,000 U.S. residents hovered around 110. After 1975, this rate increased nearly fivefold, piercing the level of 500 per 100,000 in 2006 before declining slightly to 483 in 2011.[2] Hence, in addition to being unlike other developed nations, the current U.S. incarceration rate differs greatly from the rates in years past.

Why has our incarceration rate increased so much? Why are we the world leader in prison and jail inmates per capita? This chapter addresses these questions.

Figure 2.2 Number of State and Federal Prisoners per 100,000 U.S. Residents, 1925–2011

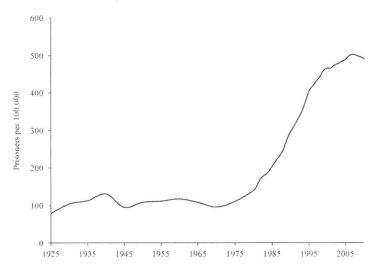

SOURCE: U.S. Department of Justice (2011).

THE DETERMINANTS OF A COUNTRY'S INCARCERATION RATE

Two broad factors determine a country's incarceration rate: 1) the rate at which people are admitted to prison, and 2) the amount of time someone admitted to prison can expect to serve. For example, if we admit 100 people per 100,000 residents per year to prison, and each person serves two years on average, we will have an incarceration rate of 200 per 100,000. Of course, the population will turn over. Each year 100 per 100,000 new admits are offset by 100 per 100,000 releases. Nonetheless, if admissions and time served are stable we can predict the level at which the incarceration rate will settle.

By extension, any factors that change either the prison admissions rate or the amount of time one can expect to serve if one is admitted to prison will change the stable incarceration rate. For example, suppose that stopping the use of lead paint in residential interiors causes a reduction in lead levels in children, increases in cognitive ability, and a permanent reduction in crime. A reduction in crime will lead to fewer admissions per year and eventually a lower incarceration rate. Alternatively, suppose we were to bring back prohibition and make alcohol sales (a previously legal activity) an offense punishable by incarceration. This increase in the scope of what we define as criminal activity would likely lead to higher annual admissions to prison, as people are still likely to drink. As a final example, suppose we pass legislation that increases effective sentence length from two years to three years. Such a change will also increase the prison population. Moreover, if we allow in our hypothetical example for multiple types of crime, with more serious crimes punished with stiffer sentences, a change in the composition of criminal activity may either increase or decrease the prison population through an effect on average time served.

As these examples illustrate, prison admissions and time served can fluctuate as a result of changes in behavior (for example, the change in crime rates caused by lead paint abatement or a shift in the

composition of crime) or changes in policy (bringing back prohibition or legislatively increasing sentencing length). This distinction is important. To the extent that crime trends are driving incarceration growth, one might characterize the patterns in Figures 2.1 and 2.2 as simply reflecting our response to a particularly severe crime problem. On the other hand, to the extent that policy choices are driving these increases, our high incarceration rate and dubious distinction as the country that uses incarceration most intensively is a product of our own choosing.

To evaluate the source of growth in U.S. incarceration rates, we will look at admissions rates and estimates of expected time served in state prisons. Figure 2.3 presents the number of prison admissions per 100,000 U.S. residents for the years 1984 and 2009.[3] The figure reveals very little change in admissions for serious violent crime,

Figure 2.3 Admissions to Prison per 100,000 U.S. Residents by Offense Type, 1984 and 2009

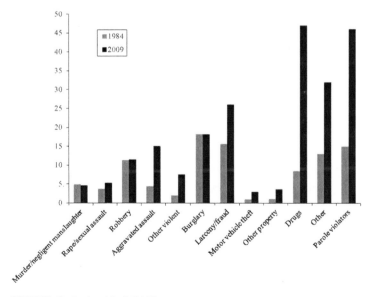

SOURCE: Raphael and Stoll (2013).

though the admissions rates for aggravated assault and other violent crime roughly quadruple. There are much larger increases, both proportionally and in absolute value, for drug offenses and for parole violations. Annual admissions for drug offenses increased more than fivefold, from 9 per 100,000 to 47 per 100,000, while the admissions rate for parole violators tripled from 15 to 46 per 100,000. We also observe sizable increases in the admission rates for larceny/fraud and the "Other" category, which generally encompasses less serious crimes.

Of course, these increases in admissions rates may be driven by either changes in crime rates or changes in sentencing and policing policy. To explore this issue, Figure 2.4 documents changes in crime rates, the rate at which given crimes are cleared by an arrest, and the rate at which arrests result in prison admissions for seven broad offense categories.[4] The crime rate trends show the extent to which higher crime rates are driving incarceration growth. The arrests per crime provide an indication of the extent to which more policing (or more effective policing) drives growth through a higher likelihood of apprehending criminal suspects. Prison admissions per arrest gauges the extent to which our sentencing system sends an offender to prison, conditional on the offender being caught for the crime committed. Hence, we can think of the first factor as behavioral (our general propensity to commit crimes and how it has changed) and the last two factors as reflecting policy choices (our policing efforts and degree to which we mete out prison sentences).

Figure 2.4 characterizes the changes in these factors by calculating the ratio of the 2009 value to the 1984 value. Ratios greater than one indicate higher values in 2009, while ratios less than one indicate lower values. The message from the figure is quite clear: essentially all of the growth in prison admissions is driven by an increase in our propensity to punish offenders with prison terms. Very little can be explained by crime trends and policing. In fact, for each of the crime rates the ratio is considerably less than one, reflecting the well-documented decline in U.S. crime rates over this period.[5] For

Figure 2.4 Crime Rates, Arrests per Crime, and Prison Admissions per Arrest in 2009 Relative to 1984 by Offense Type

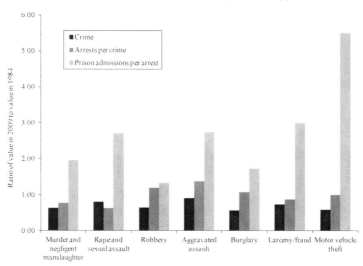

SOURCE: Raphael and Stoll (2013).

the policing variables, arrests per crime increase for a few categories (particularly robbery and burglary) but decline for many others. The ratios for prison admissions per arrest are uniformly greater than one and relatively large. For example, someone arrested for murder in 2009 is roughly twice as likely to be admitted to prison relative to a comparable arrestee in 1984. For rape and sexual assault, aggravated assault, and larceny theft, admissions per arrest increase nearly threefold. The likelihood of being sent to prison conditional on being arrested for auto theft in 2009 is five and half times the value for 1984. In essence, the higher admissions rates are explained entirely by the higher chances of being sent to prison if arrested.

It is also the case that the amount of time that a convicted felon can expect to serve for given offenses has increased over this period, especially for serious violent crime. Figure 2.5 presents estimates of how much time a prison inmate admitted to a state prison can expect

Figure 2.5 Time Served, by Offense, 1984 and 2009

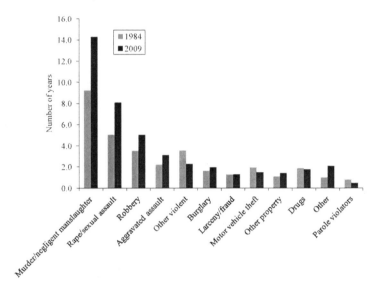

SOURCE: Raphael and Stoll (2013).

to serve in 1984 and 2009, by offense. For murder and sexual assault, there are large increases in time served on the order of five additional years for murder and three additional years for rape/sexual assault. We also see increases in expected time served for robbery and aggravated assault, though of smaller magnitude. Sentences for drug crime and property offenses among state inmates appear to be relatively stable over this period. We should note, however, that in the federal prison system, sentences for drug offenders increased appreciably over this period.

Raphael and Stoll (2013) use the statistics in these figures to simulate what the U.S. incarceration rate would have been had we not increased our propensity to punish offenders with prison and not increased sentence lengths. This exercise reveals that nearly all incarceration growth both in state and federal prisons is explained by tougher sentencing policy. There are some subtle differences between the state and the federal prison systems. Harsher punishment for drug offenders explains the lion's share of growth in the federal prison population but a smaller though still significant portion of the growth in state prison populations. On the other hand, longer sentences for violent offenders is a particularly important determinant of growth in state prisons but less so among federal prisoners.

These details aside, harsher sentencing policies certainly explain the growth in incarceration rates as well as the United States' position along this dimension relative to the rest of the world. The next section discusses these sentencing policy changes.[6]

SPECIFIC POLICY CHANGES DRIVING INCARCERATION GROWTH

Given the decentralized nature of U.S. corrections, it is somewhat difficult to completely characterize the full list of sentencing reforms that explain increasing incarceration rates over the past three decades. With 51 effective legislative bodies actively reforming 51 separate penal codes and sentencing structures, such a list would be extremely long and somewhat difficult to digest. Nonetheless, there have been broad policy trends in sentencing practices observed in most states that have driven the increases in admissions rates and time served documented above. Here we highlight some of these trends.[7]

To start, sentencing has become considerably more structured, with less discretion afforded to parole boards and prison authorities to determine prisoner release dates. Prior to the prison boom, all states operated under indeterminate sentencing systems, whereby judges assigned minimum and maximum sentences with a wide gulf between the two. Prison parole boards had broad discretion to determine actual time served based on behavior while incarcerated, efforts and progress toward rehabilitation, and formal and perhaps informal assessments of recidivism risk. In the years since, many states have moved to determinate sentencing systems, where judges hand down a single sentence and actual time served is determined largely by administrative rules pertaining to "good time" credits that inmates earn against their sentences.

Concurrently, state legislatures as well as the federal government enacted numerous mandatory minimum sentences that specified minimum amounts of time to be served for specific crimes as well as for crimes with specific aggravating circumstances. In many instances, these mandatory minimums were targeted at specific violent crimes, including but not limited to car-jacking, crimes against children, and premeditated murder. However, there are many instances of stiff mandatory minimum sentences for less serious offenses, with drug crime a particularly salient example. One mandatory minimum sentence that has received considerable attention is the prescribed punishment assigned in federal courts for crack cocaine violations. These laws, created by direct acts of Congress during the mid to late 1980s, specified very long sentences for crimes involving relatively small amounts of crack cocaine. In particular, these laws created a 100-to-1 sentencing ratio for crime involving similar quantities of crack and powder cocaine despite the identical chemical composition and psychopharmacological effects of the two drugs. In 2010, federal sentencing policy was amended to reduce this disparity, but it stopped far short of equalizing sentences for crack and powder cocaine (reducing the sentencing ratio from 100-to-1 to 18-to-1).

Many states also passed laws mandating sentence enhancements for repeat offenders, usually under the moniker of "three strikes and you're out." Such laws enhance sentences for convicted offenders with prior felonies, with the most stringent mandating sentences of 20 years to life for minor crimes that constitute third felony strikes. California was one of the earliest states to adopt such a law and, until recently, mandated some of the toughest penalties for second and third strikers regardless of the nature of the recent offense.[8]

As a final example, during the 1990s nearly all states passed some form of "truth-in-sentencing" law mandating that prison inmates serve a minimum portion of their sentences (usually 85 percent). Through prison construction subsidies, the federal government included explicit incentives for states to implement such legislation in the 1994 Violent Crime Control and Law Enforcement Act. While research on this topic tends to find that most of the states would have adopted such laws regardless of the federal incentives, the 1994 crime bill did increase the average time served provision (as the construction subsidy requires 85 percent time-served requirements) and thus contributed to growth in time served during the 1990s (see Sabol et al. 2002).

There is broad agreement that changes in sentencing practices led to growth in the U.S. incarceration rate. There is perhaps less consensus about why sentencing practices changed so drastically beginning around 1975. Some scholars tie the shift toward more punitive sentencing to the aftermath of the Civil Rights movement and the national political strategy of the Republican Party to appeal to disaffected southern white voters (Weaver 2007). Others attribute the shift to a change in consensus around 1970 regarding the effectiveness (or more precisely, the ineffectiveness) of efforts to rehabilitate offenders (Wilsou 1975). Other scholars point to the asymmetric nature of political competitions involving crime control. It is politically safe to advocate for "tough-on-crime" policies. On the other hand, advocating for moderation, deliberation, and consideration of benefits and costs in sentencing policy puts one out on a limb politically. While it is difficult to formally distinguish between these alternative theses, it is inarguable that over the past three decades, sentencing policy has become highly politicized. While prison sentences and time served previously were determined by judges and parole boards, sentencing is now determined by specific state and federal legislative acts. Moreover, the content of this legislation is often hashed out in highly politicized settings by legislators with little expertise in criminal justice policy.

IMPLICATIONS FOR THE EMPLOYMENT
OF FORMER PRISONERS

The rise in the U.S. incarceration rate and our position as the country with the highest incarceration rate in the world has little to do with our propensity to commit crime and everything to do with our chosen sentencing policies. We currently incarcerate our citizens at rates that are unprecedented. This incarceration boom has left in its wake a large population of former prison inmates who have spent some of their most productive years in prison and then cycled in and out of prisons and jails before effectively aging out of the criminal justice system. These individuals face stigma in the labor market and create unique challenges to employers who may or may not be willing to hire them.

Notes

1. Here I present total incarceration rates due to the fact that other countries do not draw a sharp distinction between jail and prison inmates. Moreover, the International Centre for Prison Studies includes pretrial populations in their international comparisons, as in many nations many may serve relatively lengthy incarceration spells while awaiting trial. (See http://www.prisonstudies.org/ [accessed November 6, 2013]).
2. The difference between the U.S. incarceration rates in Figures 2.1 and 2.2 is due to the fact that in the international comparison jail inmates are included in the calculations. We do not have data on the jail incarceration rate that date back to 1925. However, between 1980 and 2011, the jail incarceration rate increased from 80 to 242 per 100,000 U.S. residents (Minton 2013; Raphael and Stoll 2013).
3. The earliest year for which the necessary data are available to be able to break down admission rates by offense is 1984. See Raphael and Stoll (2013, Chapter 2) for a detailed discussion of these data.
4. Multiplying these three rates gives us the overall admissions rate for a given crime. To see this fact, note that the crime rate is given by the ratio crimes/population, the crime clearance rate is given by the ratio arrests/crimes, and the conditional admissions rate is given by the ratio prison admissions/arrests. The product of these three ratios, crimes/population × arrests/crimes × prison admissions/arrests, simply equals prison

admissions/population. Hence, these three ratios allow us to decompose the prison admissions rate into the behavioral component (crime rates) and the two factors that depend roughly on the effectiveness of policing and sentencing policy.

5. Comparable ratios for drug crime are noticeably absent from the figure. This is due to the fact that there is no "drug crime" total to use as a basis, while for the crime categories in Figure 2.4 we can employ crimes reported to police to estimate crime rates. Regarding drugs, it is possible to assess trends in drug arrest rates and trends in admissions per arrest. Both factors are likely influenced by enforcement policy, though changes in drug use and trafficking behavior are likely to surface in changes in arrest rates. Raphael and Stoll (2013) document very large increases in the rate at which drug arrests result in a prison admission over this period.

6. We are not the only scholars to take a hard look at prison admissions data and come to this conclusion. In an earlier analysis, Blumstein and Beck (1999) conclude that nearly all incarceration growth can be explained by changes in official sentencing at the punishment stage of the court processing flow. In a more recent analysis, Neal and Rick (2014) estimate how the entire distribution of sentences has changed within specifically defined crime categories, and show a notable increase in the severity of sentencing.

7. For a detailed exposition and listing of sentencing reforms occurring in the United States over the past three decades, see Stemen, Rengifo, and Wilson (2006).

8. In 2012, California voters approved a ballot initiative that scales back the three strikes sentences for repeat offenders convicted of relatively less serious felonies.

Chapter 3

A Portrait of Future, Current, and Former Prison Inmates

F ormer prison inmates face a number of challenges in procuring and maintaining stable employment. Those who go to prison are hardly a representative cross section of the U.S. adult population. They are overwhelmingly male, have low levels of educational attainment, and have relatively low levels of formal work experience for their age. They also tend to come from poverty, suffer disproportionately from mental health problems as well as substance abuse problems, and come from minority groups with historically poor outcomes in the labor market.

Aside from the stigmatizing or psychologically and physiologically damaging effects of prison, this portrait in and of itself suggests that those who serve time in the United States face a number of personal challenges in the labor market that are independent of their criminal histories yet aggravated by interactions with the criminal justice system. In other words, employer preferences aside, many individuals who serve prison time are likely to perform poorly in the labor market because of their personal characteristics and socioeconomic histories. This chapter presents an empirical portrait of who serves time in the United States.

To provide a complete description, I present tabulations of nationally representative data sets that characterize future prison inmates, current prison inmates, and former prison inmates. By future prison inmates, I am referring to youth who we know through observation over time end up in an adult correctional facility at some point in the future. By current inmates I am referring to the stock of those incarcerated at a specific point in time. While we do not have nationally representative surveys that permit identification of the pool of former inmates, national data are available on individuals that are released

27

from prison in any given year. Together, these three sources of data permit a comprehensive assessment of the characteristics and personal histories that former prison inmates bring to the labor market, which, in many instances, likely hampers their job searches and, more generally, their employment prospects.

FUTURE PRISON INMATES

It is hard to predict who among today's youth will serve time in an adult correctional institution. Many who engage in delinquent behavior will age out of crime and go on to lead crime-free conventional adult lives. Some who do not get into trouble as youth will commit felonies as adults and serve time as a result. Moreover, being prosecuted, convicted, and incarcerated as a youth appears to have an independent causal effect on the likelihood that one serves time as an adult.[1] Hence, local criminal justice policy in the jurisdiction where one grows up may have lasting effects on one's future involvement with the criminal justice system.

These caveats aside, there are indeed certain personal and family background characteristics that emerge at an early age and that signal high risk of future criminal involvement and incarceration. In particular, early criminal activity, growing up in poverty, growing up in single-parent households, and poor grades are among these characteristics. In this section, we document how those youth who go on to serve time as an adult differ from youth who do not.

The U.S. Bureau of Labor Statistics has an ongoing effort to collect data for a cohort of individuals who were between the ages of 12 and 16 in 1996. The 1997 National Longitudinal Survey of Youth (NLSY) has collected data on these individuals for each year from 1997 through 2010, including detailed information on criminal justice involvement, employment history, family background characteristics, educational attainment, and various measures of delinquent behavior. Using this data set, I identify all individuals who served at least six months in an adult institution by 2010 (when the individuals in the data sample are between 26 and 30 years of age). I then compare various characteristics of those with an observable incarceration event to those without.[2] Table 3.1 presents a comparison of some basic demographic and family background characteristics. The table first presents tabulations for females and then for males. Most of the figures reflect averages as of the first survey date during the year 1997. Among both genders, African American youth are disproportionately represented among those who will eventually serve time, especially among males. Over

Table 3.1 Demographic Characteristics of Youth in 1997 Who Are Eventually Incarcerated by 2010 and Youth Who Are Not

	Females		Males	
	No incarceration history	Incarceration history	No incarceration history	Incarceration history
Age	14.31	14.67	14.31	14.41
Race/ethnicity (%)				
Non-Hispanic, white	67.41	64.13	67.43	49.05
Non-Hispanic, black	15.44	26.80	14.18	34.38
Non-Hispanic, other	4.87	0.00	5.04	1.40
Hispanic	12.28	9.07	13.36	13.36
Percent poor	13.40	30.10	11.80	26.20
Income as a percent of the poverty line	313.00	143.58	324.12	204.55
Mother's education	12.85	12.19	12.92	11.97
Father's education	12.98	11.28	13.05	11.44
Mother's age at birth of respondent	25.16	23.00	25.93	23.51
Percent residing with both biological parents at				
Age 2	49.16	14.60	53.43	19.66
Age 6	48.34	7.40	52.94	18.86
Age 12	47.98	6.83	52.61	19.30
The 1997 interview	51.34	11.15	55.49	24.48

SOURCE: Author's tabulations from the NLSY97.

34 percent of the young men who will serve time in this sample are black, while the comparable figure for those who do not is 14 percent. The likelihood of living in a household below the poverty line is also discretely higher among youth who eventually serve time. Among young women, those who serve time are roughly 2.3 times more likely to be living in poverty in 1997 (30.1 percent for those who do time relative to 13.4 percent for those who do not); among young men, the comparable figure is 2.2 times. The ratio of household income to the poverty line is also discretely lower among future inmates.

We also observe several important differences in the characteristics of the youth's parents. Those who eventually serve time are on average born to younger mothers, with a difference in maternal age at birth of roughly two years among both male and female youth. Moreover, the educational attainment of biological mothers and fathers is lower on average among future inmates by roughly a year to a year and a half. Finally, youth who eventually serve time are considerably less likely to be residing with both biological parents. This is true at ages, 2, 6, 12, and the youth's age as of the 1997 initial interview.

Table 3.2 continues this comparison with a focus on school performance, ultimate educational attainment, and evidence of early delinquent behavior. With the exception of ultimate educational attainment (which is measured as of 2010), all measures reflect youth outcomes at the beginning of this longitudinal data study. I have grouped youth into three categories according to their self-reported grades in the 8th grade: 1) those reporting receiving mostly F's, mostly D's, and D's and C's; 2) those receiving C's and B's; and 3) those receiving A's and B's. The differences in academic performance are particularly striking. Among males, roughly 34 percent perform in the lowest category among those with an incarceration future, while 50 percent are in the middle category. The comparable figures for young men who do not serve prison time are 14 and 38 percent, respectively. Young women tend to report better 8th grade outcomes than their male counterparts. However, we still observe poorer grades among those females who eventually serve time. Not surprisingly, there are large

Table 3.2 Academic Performance, Eventual Educational Attainment, and Self-Reported Delinquent Behavior in 1997 of Youth Who Are Eventually Incarcerated by 2010 and Youth Who Are Not (%)

	Females		Males	
	No incarceration history	Incarceration history	No incarceration history	Incarceration history
Typical grades in 8th grade				
F's, D's, D's and C's	8.57	14.92	13.85	34.02
C's, C's and B's	29.90	47.87	37.62	50.33
B's, B's and A's, A's	61.52	37.21	48.54	15.66
Education as of 2010				
<High school	13.31	33.47	15.24	54.81
High school grad.	23.12	37.00	27.71	28.23
Some college	25.25	29.53	26.47	15.75
College grad.	38.33	0.00	30.58	1.21
Self-reported delinquent behavior in 1997				
Ever smoked	42.7	74.2	40.8	65.0
Ever drink alcohol	44.5	58.6	45.7	58.4
Ever use marijuana	19.9	49.6	21.6	41.6
Ever carry a gun	3.1	19.9	15.7	31.7
Ever a member of a gang	3.4	11.9	5.6	13.5
Ever destroy property	20.4	40.1	36.7	51.9
Ever stolen something worth <$50	30.0	42.9	37.9	54.4
Ever stolen something worth >$50	5.2	21.2	9.6	27.9
Ever commit other property crime	3.2	15.4	13.3	28.4
Ever attack someone	12.8	37.3	21.8	44.6
Ever sell drugs	5.7	12.5	8.2	18.0

SOURCE: Author's tabulations from the NLSY97.

differences in ultimate educational attainment between those who serve time and those who do not. Among men, roughly 55 percent of those who eventually serve time have less than a high school degree by 2010 while only 1 percent has a college degree. The comparable figures among those who do not serve time are 15 and 31 percent, respectively. Again, women ultimately outperform men in terms of educational attainment. However, we still observe relatively worse outcomes among young women with a future incarceration.

Finally, there are large differences in self-reported delinquent behavior in 1997 between those who are ultimately incarcerated and those who are not. For example, young men who go to prison by 2010 are 25 percentage points more likely to have smoked cigarettes, 13 percentage points more likely to have used alcohol, 20 percentage points more likely to have tried marijuana, and 16 percentage points more likely to indicate that they have ever carried a gun. There are also notable differences in self-reported engagement in property crime, having assaulted someone, and having sold drugs. We observe a similar and uniformly higher propensity to engage in delinquent behavior among young women who eventually serve time.

As a final comparison, Figures 3.1 and 3.2 document differences in cumulative years of work experience beyond age 20 as of the 2010 interview. As the members of the sample are between 26 and 30 years of age, each individual could potentially have 6–10 years of work experience by this final interview round. The figures show the percentage of either no-future incarceration or future incarceration groups with various levels of cumulative work experience for females (Figure 3.1) and males (Figure 3.2). Again, the differences are striking. Those with a future incarceration are relatively concentrated among the low experience categories. For example, among future male inmates, fully one-fifth have accumulated less than one year of work experience by 2010, compared with 10 percent of those who do not go to prison. Moreover, we see relatively few former inmates among those with high levels of work experience. The patterns for women are generally the same. As an overall summary, average cumulative work experience by 2010 among young men with future incarceration is 4.2 years. This is 2.25 years lower than the average

Figure 3.1 Distribution of Total Years of Work Experience among Female NLSY97 Respondents by the 2010 Interview

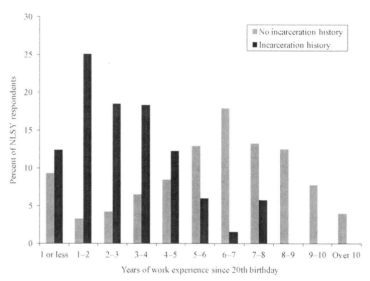

SOURCE: Author's tabulations from the NLSY97.

for those who never go and amounts to 65 percent of work experience levels for men who are never incarcerated. The differences for women are larger. Among those who do time, women accumulate 2.9 years of work experience by 2010, fully 3.2 years less than their nonincarcerated counterparts. Moreover, cumulative experience among future female inmates is less than half that of women who do not serve time.

In summary, this portrait of future inmates is relatively bleak. These young people are more likely to grow up in poverty, have parents with indicators of low socioeconomic status, engage in early criminal and delinquent behavior, and perform poorly in school at a young age. Perhaps most relevant for a book on the employment consequences of doing time, there are very large differences in cumulative work experience.

Figure 3.2 Distribution of Total Years of Work Experience among Male NLSY97 Respondents by the 2010 Interview

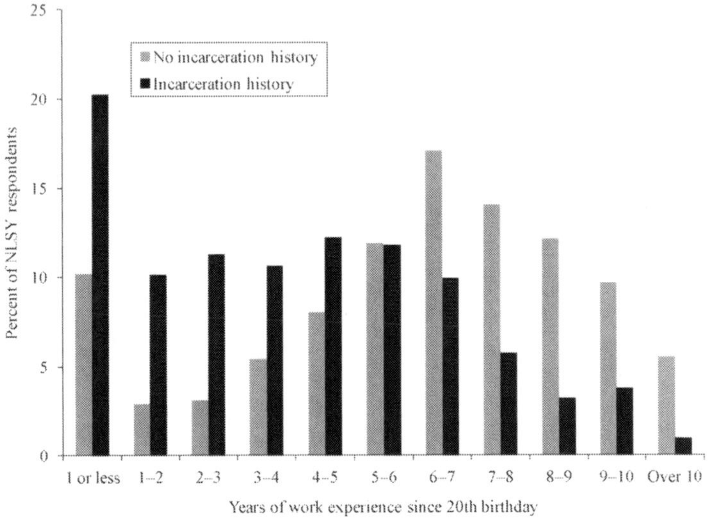

SOURCE: Author's tabulations from the NLSY97.

CURRENT PRISON INMATES

Our characterization of which teenagers will eventually go to prison will differ from the stock of prison inmates at any given time for a number of reasons. First, the current NLSY data set only follows youth through 2010 when they reach 26–30 years of age. Many people enter prison at older ages, especially in recent years with the general expansion of the country's use of prison as punishment. Hence, our characterization of future inmates is partial and likely misses many who will eventually do time.

Second, a snapshot of the prison population at a specific point in time is more likely to capture people who are serving relatively long sentences. This will alter the age profile, the offense profile, and many other characteristics of the current population of prison inmates relative to future and past prison inmates. Finally, the current population of inmates is more likely to capture individuals who offend repeatedly, serially violate parole, and generally serve multiple spells in prison.

The stock of current prison inmates provides the pool of individuals that will eventually be released back into noninstitutionalized society. It is notable that roughly 95 percent of current inmates will eventually be released, with the overwhelming majority to be released within the next three years. Hence, the characteristics of the current prison population are in many ways reflective of the nation's reentry caseload and the incumbent challenges that service providers and their clients will face.

Table 3.3 provides an empirical portrait of the stock of state and federal prison inmates as of 2004.[3] In many ways, the population characteristics parallel what we saw among future prison inmates. Prison inmates in the United States are overwhelmingly male (over 90 percent in both state and federal prisons). The majority of prison inmates are high school dropouts, with much lower levels of educational attainment among state prisoners relative to federal prisons. Racial and ethnic minorities are heavily overrepresented. African Americans, who constitute 12 percent of the U.S. adult population, make up 43 percent of the state prison population and 46 percent of the federal prison population. Similarly, Hispanics, who constitute 13 percent of the U.S. adult population, make up 18 percent of the state prison population and 25 percent of federal prisoners.

Considering the typical age-offending trajectory, inmates are relatively old. It is a well-known fact that criminal offending declines strongly with age, with the highest offending levels occurring during the late teen years and declining quickly thereafter. Even among prison inmates, serious behavioral violations while incarcerated decline at a fast rate with age (Raphael and Stoll 2013, Chapter 7). We observe in Table 3.3 that the age of the median state prisoner is 34, while the comparable figure for federal prisoners is 35. Hence, among

Table 3.3 Characteristics of State and Federal Prisoners in 2004

	State prisoners	Federal prisoners
Male (%)	93.2	92.9
Education attainment (%)		
Less than high school	66.6	55.7
High school graduate	19.5	21.4
More than high school	13.9	22.7
Hispanic (%)	18.2	25.1
Race (%)		
White	48.7	43.3
Black	43.0	46.0
Other	8.3	10.7
Median age	34	35
Median age at first arrest	17	18
Median age at first crime	14	14
Has manic depression/bipolar disorder (%)	9.7	4.1
Has schizophrenia (%)	4.6	1.9
Ever attempted suicide (%)	12.9	5.9
Homeless prior to arrest (%)	8.6	3.7
Controlling offense (%)		
Violent	47.9	14.6
Property	18.2	4.1
Drugs	21.3	55.2
Weapons/other	12.6	26.0

SOURCE: U.S. Department of Justice (2004).
NOTE: Some totals do not sum to 100 because of rounding.

current prison inmates, we are likely observing individuals paying the consequences for criminal activity during their younger years. Regarding the other age indicators, those serving time for prison self-report initial criminal activity and arrest at very young ages. For both federal and state prisoners, the median age when one first commits a crime is 14. Moreover, the median inmate in both systems is arrested by his or her 18th birthday.

The prevalence of severe mental illness is particularly high among prison inmates, especially state prison inmates. Roughly 10 percent of state prison inmates and 4 percent of federal prison inmates suffer from manic depression/bipolar disorder. While estimates for the general population vary, existing studies place the prevalence of this disease among U.S. adults at between 1.6 and 4.0 percent.[4] Hence, among state prisoners (the lion's share of prisoners in the United States), the prevalence of bipolar disorder is 2.2–5.6 times the comparable rate for the general adult population.

The relative prevalence of schizophrenia is particularly high, with 4.6 percent of state prison inmates and 1.9 percent of federal inmates reporting ever being diagnosed with the disease. With the prevalence rate among the general adult population ranging from 0.6 to 0.7 percent, the rate among state prisoners is 6.5–7.5 times that for the average adult, while the rate among federal inmates is 2.5–3.0 times that of the general adult population. Given the high rates of mental illness, it is not surprising that a sizable percentage of prison inmates have attempted suicide in the past and were homeless at the time of the arrest leading to their current incarceration.

The final rows of Table 3.3 show the broad categories of offenses for which current prison inmates are being incarcerated. These figures are particularly useful for comparison against inmates released in a given year. Hence we highlight these facts here. Slightly less than half of state prison inmates are incarcerated for a violent offense and a fifth for property offenses. In state prisons, 21 percent are serving time for drug offenses, while those in the balance are serving time for other crimes. This distribution contrasts sharply with that for the federal prison system. Fully 55 percent of federal prisoners in 2004 are doing time for a drug offense, while 26 percent are doing time for federal weapons offenses and other offenses. Given the surge in federal inmates incarcerated for immigration offenses, the proportion in the "Other" category will certainly be higher when the next representative survey of federal inmates is released.

FORMER PRISON INMATES

Ideally, one would like to see data for a nationally representative sample of U.S. adults who have been incarcerated at some point in the past. As we discussed in Chapter 2, the population of former prison inmates is much larger than the population of current prison inmates or the flow of prison releases in any given year. As a sizable portion of released inmates (roughly 40 percent) will never set foot in a prison again, and among those who do many will eventually desist from crime, the size of the former populations has grown commensurate with the incarceration rate.

Unfortunately, none of the major household surveys fielded in the United States, such as the Current Population Survey or the American Community Survey, inquire about the criminal histories of the respondents. Hence, estimating the size of the former inmate population has required the use of demographic forecasting techniques and other creative research strategies.

The United States does collect data on state prison inmates admitted to and released from prison each year, and the degree of coverage is such that the data can be used to generate a fairly accurate description of recent releases. This information is useful in that those recently released from prisons are those who are likely to show up on employers' doorsteps with little experience in negotiating the labor market with their new status as "former prison inmate." Furthermore, labor market intermediaries serving the former inmate population will largely be representing those recently released rather than individuals who over time have become more established in the noninstitutionalized world.

Table 3.4 presents some basic descriptive statistics for state prison inmates released in 2003. We pick this particular year because it is close to the survey year for the stock of inmates and thus the reader can make comparisons between those in prison at a given point in time and those being released. Similar to the stock of prison inmates, state prison releases in 2003 are overwhelmingly male and dispropor-

Table 3.4   Characteristics of Prisoners Released from State Prison in 2003

Demographic characteristics (%)	
Male	89.7
White	46.4
Black	51.9
Hispanic	20.2
Educational attainment (%)	
Less than high school	53.7
12th/GED	38.7
More than high school	7.6
Median age	32
Time served on current term (months)	
25th percentile	11.3
50th percentile	20.8
75th percentile	39.9
Conditionally released to parole or some other form of community corrections supervision (%)	73.9
Prior felony incarceration (%)	32.7
Controlling offense (%)	
Violent	24.5
Property	30.5
Drugs	32.1
Weapons/other	12.8

SOURCE: National Archive of Criminal Justice Data (2003).

tionately minority. In addition, formal educational attainment is quite low, with the majority having less than a high school degree and a very small percent with anything more than a high school education. Released prisoners are generally younger than the stock of prison inmates, with a difference in median age of two years. In addition, the median inmate is being released after serving 21 months in a state prison. Their total time served may be considerably longer once pre-trial jail detention is taken into account, but we are unable to observe this in this data set.

Although not shown in the table, inmates being released from incarceration spells caused by a parole violation may have served very short terms, many for less than six months. However, such inmates certainly had terms in prison preceding their parole violations longer than their current terms. This can be seen in part by the fact that roughly one-third of the released inmates have at least one felony incarceration before the term from which they are being released. The overwhelming majority of released prison inmates are conditionally released to state parole authorities or some other form of community corrections. This essentially means that most of the inmates face various restrictions and can have their conditional release from prison revoked should they violate any of the terms of their parole. Many cannot leave their county of residence while on parole, many face random visits from parole officers, and most must meet with their parole officers on a regular basis. Of course, many will be subject to random drug testing. Finally, many will be returned to prison or face short spells in county jails for behavioral infractions that would not result in the incarceration of someone not on probation or parole.

The final set of figures shows the offenses for which releases were incarcerated. In contrast to the stock of prison inmates, only one-quarter of prison releases have served time for violent offenses, while 30 percent served time for property offenses and 32 percent served time for a drug offense. Recall that half of current inmates are serving time for a violent offense, while roughly two-fifths are serving time for property and drug crimes (one-fifth for each offense category). These differences reflect an important fact about the prison boom of the last three decades and the differential implications for the stock of both current and former inmates: longer sentences for violent crime and the higher propensity to punish relatively low level offenders with prison has on net led to only a small decline in the proportion of current inmates serving time for violent crimes. In other words, even though we are admitting individuals for drug and property crimes at historic rates, the sentences for violent crime have increased by enough to keep their relative representation of violent criminals among the incarcerated constant.

That being said, those who serve relatively short sentences are heavily overrepresented among those released from prison, and by extension, among those in noninstitutionalized society who have served time in the past. Hence, those with felony drug and property crime convictions likely contribute the most to growth in the population of former prison inmates (as is reflected in their relatively disproportionate representation among those released from prison).

IMPLICATIONS FOR THE EMPLOYMENT OF FORMER PRISONERS

Our empirical portrait of future, current, and former prison inmates is quite bleak. The members of this overwhelmingly male and minority population face a number of issues that likely limit their employment prospects independently of any stigmatizing effect associated with their criminal histories. They have very low levels of formal educational attainment and performed poorly in school at young ages, suggesting that their academic aptitudes are likely below the average for those at the level at which they stopped their formal schooling. Many have extensive criminal histories that extend back to young ages. Formal work experience is low relative to others their age. In sum, many of these individuals would face problems in the labor market absent any stigmatizing effect of having a criminal history record and a history of incarceration.

Notes

1. For an excellent empirical analysis of the effects of juvenile incarceration on future criminal activity see Aizer and Doyle (2013).
2. I also produced these tabulations defining the incarcerated as those who serve any time in an adult correctional facility. The results look quite similar. I chose to focus on those serving at least six months to exclude individuals who spend very short amounts of time in an adult jail from the incarceration-history group.
3. The most recently available year for this survey is 2004.
4. See Kessler, Bergland, et al. (2005) and Kessler, McGonagle, et al. (1994) for estimates of the prevalence of mental illness in the general adults population.

Chapter 4

Employers' Perceptions
of Former Inmates

In the previous chapter we reviewed the many personal characteristics of former prison inmates that likely limit their employment prospects. In addition to very low levels of formal education, many have low levels of cumulative work experience relative to other adults their age, have histories of substance abuse, often lack the soft skills needed in modern workplaces, and suffer disproportionately from severe mental illness. Of course, within the low-wage labor market, there are many adults without official criminal histories who have similar demographic profiles and thus face similar limitations. Former inmates, however, face additional barriers to employment that are created specifically by their officially recorded criminal pasts.

Put simply, employers have legitimate reasons to be cautious about hiring former inmates, and more generally, individual applicants with criminal convictions. Moreover, risk-averse employers may overestimate the risks associated with hiring former prison inmates, especially those employers who have little experience with this population. Taken together, perceptions on the demand side of the labor market regarding specific risks associated with an applicant's criminal record, whether justified or not, certainly limits the employment opportunities available to former prison inmates, compounding the effects of the barriers created by their own demographics.

This employer reluctance creates obstacles to progress in a number of policy domains that are of first-order importance in the United States. First, given the extreme racial disparities in involvement with the criminal justice system, the demand-side barriers to employment most certainly have disparate impacts on African Americans, and African American males in particular. Hence, such barriers likely exacerbate racial inequality in the United States emanating from racial inequality in employment and compensation.

Second, with such a large population of former prison inmates among noninstitutionalized U.S. adults, a general reluctance of employers to hire former prison inmates likely relegates these individuals to the most menial jobs with the lowest pay. By extension, the circumscribed employment opportunity set is likely to deepen poverty among these individuals as well as their dependents. As incarceration is an outcome that is generally experienced by the poor, the incidence of this income decline hits families, households, and individuals, who are already at the bottom of the socioeconomic ladder.

In this chapter, I discuss the demand side of the labor market for former inmates. In particular, I review what we know about employer perceptions pertaining to ex-offenders and the likely reasons for their extreme reluctance to hire former inmates. I also discuss the increasing use of criminal history records in screening potential applicants and the policy initiative within this domain. Finally, I review what we know about actual hiring outcomes that are driven by the stigma associated with a criminal past.

WHAT DO EMPLOYERS THINK ABOUT EX-OFFENDERS?

Figure 4.1 presents the results from a survey of California employers carried out in 2003. The survey samples all business and nonprofit establishments with at least five employees excluding government agencies, public schools or universities, and establishments in either the agricultural, forestry, or fisheries industries. The survey design was such that employers who do more hiring are given more weight in the tabulations, and thus the sentiments described are representative of what the average job seeker in California in 2003 was likely to encounter.

Employers were queried about their general willingness to hire applicants with various characteristics. Figure 4.1 displays responses for three characteristics generally perceived to be a negative on an applicant's resume: a criminal conviction, being unemployed for a

Figure 4.1 How Willing Would You Be to Accept an Applicant with Various Characteristics? California Employers Respond

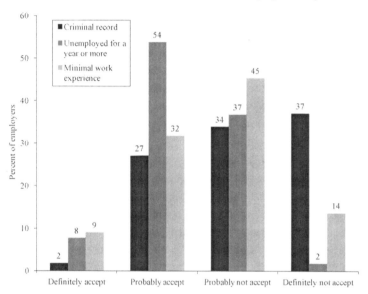

SOURCE: Institute for Research on Labor and Employment (2007).

year or more, and having little formal work experience. The figure shows general reluctance to hire workers with each of these traits. For example, less than 10 percent of employers indicate that they would definitely hire such applicants. However, employers exhibit the greatest reluctance to hire workers with criminal histories. For example, 71 percent of employers indicate that they would probably not or definitely not hire an applicant with a criminal history. The comparable figure for an applicant who has been unemployed for year or more is 39 percent, while the figure for an applicant with little work experience is 59 percent. Furthermore, there is research suggesting that relative to actual hiring practices, employers overstate their hypothetical willingness to hire applicants with criminal convictions (see Pager and Quillian [2005]).

While these results pertain to employers in California, the general reluctance of employers to hire applicants with criminal history records has been documented in surveys of employers in Atlanta, Boston, Detroit, Milwaukee, New York, and in several surveys of employers in Los Angeles (see Holzer, Raphael, and Stoll [2006a,b; 2007]; Pager [2007]; and Pager, Western, and Bonikowski [2009]). While there are no nationally representative employer surveys that ask these questions, the consistency across cities suggests that this reluctance is generally widespread among U.S. employers. What drives this wariness?

There certainly are many legitimate concerns that employers may raise in considering whether to hire a former prison inmate, or more generally, an applicant with prior criminal convictions. To start, many employers purchase insurance to hedge against risk created by dishonest acts by their employees. Employees with criminal histories are often deemed "not bondable" by private insurers due to the elevated risk associated with a criminal history. There is a federal bonding program that provides temporary employee-dishonesty insurance for ex-offenders that can often facilitate private purchase of such insurance following six months without incident under federal bonding.[1] However, the added paperwork and the general salience of the issue created by the inability to initially procure private insurance may be enough to tip the employer's hiring decision toward the worker without a criminal history.

Aside from perceived heightened risk of loss due to employee theft and dishonesty, employers face a liability risk associated with any harm that an employee may inflict upon a customer in the course of carrying out one's job or as a result of interactions with a customer originating at work. To the extent that the harm to the customer was foreseeable given the worker's criminal history, employers may be held liable for damages under the negligent hiring doctrine. Such concerns are certainly a driver in the increasing use of formal criminal history background checks by employers (an issue we will discuss in the next section). In light of these concerns, it is not too surprising that the surveys discussed above consistently find that those employers hiring workers into jobs that involve substantial contact with customers are the least willing to consider workers with criminal histories as acceptable applicants.

Beyond potential liability and the risk of loss through theft, some employers are legally proscribed from hiring employees with certain felonies by federal and state law, and in some instances by local ordinance. For example, employers in transportation, material handling, private security firms, financial services, health services firms working with vulnerable populations, and employers of all sorts that serve children face criminal history restrictions in whom they can hire. Moreover, such employers must exhibit due diligence in screening out unacceptable applicants.[2]

Finally, employers may simply be unwilling to hire workers with criminal records because of concerns regarding honesty and integrity and perhaps a moral aversion to people who have proven untrustworthy in the past. Technically, the U.S. Equal Employment Opportunity Commission (EEOC) argues that employers cannot categorically exclude ex-offenders from consideration for reasons that are not materially related to the ability of the applicant in question to perform the job. Nonetheless, employers are human and are likely to act on internal preferences and beliefs when making hiring decisions.

HOW DO EMPLOYERS FIND OUT ABOUT AN APPLICANT'S CRIMINAL HISTORY RECORD?

Given the liability concerns of employers and the general wariness of applicants with criminal history records, one might reasonably wonder how employers procure information about past crimes and how this information is considered in the screening and hiring process. This is a complicated and thorny issue that touches on a number of policy domains, including public safety, access to sensitive personal information by noncriminal justice users, subtle forms of discrimination that may occur in the absence of reliable criminal history records, and what can reasonably be considered by employers in hiring and screening applicants and when.

Perhaps a good place to begin this discussion is with the criminal justice information infrastructure that exists in the United States and the nature of the records that lie within. As most criminal offenses are prosecuted through state courts, nearly all records of arrests, convictions, and postconviction sentencing are maintained by county courts throughout the country. As these "criminal justice transactions" are recorded on public blotters, this information is generally considered public information and thus is open to public query.

Each county reports this information to central state criminal history repositories usually maintained by the office of the state attorney general. These state repositories serve the working needs of law enforcement in the state (they are the sources of "rap sheets" for officers in the field) as well as facilitate background checking. Although the public can access records through individual county courts, access to state criminal history repositories varies considerably from state to state, with some states, such as Florida, having relatively open access to noncriminal justice users, and other states, such as California, allowing much more restrictive access. A key difference between the records maintained by courts and those in state repositories concerns the method of identification, and thus the specific input to the query. Whereas county court records are usually searched by name with secondary confirmation by considering other factors such as race, gender, and birth date, state repositories use specific unique criminal codes linked to full sets of digitally scanned fingerprints. This alternative identification system generally leads to more accurate identification, especially for individuals with common names.

Finally, the Federal Bureau of Investigation maintains a database called the Interstate Identification Index (III) that contains information from all criminal history repositories in the country along with data on federal arrests, convictions, and sentences. Access to this database for noncriminal justice users can be authorized by state legislation and the authorization of the U.S. attorney general. The III is often queried by employers who serve vulnerable populations and employers who are legally proscribed from hiring certain types of ex-offenders.

Employers have three broad options for screening the criminal history records of their applicants that can be employed either in conjunction or isolation. First, they can simply ask. While recent years have witnessed increasing restrictions on the ability of employers to inquire about criminal histories on applications, many employers still simply ask up front about criminal history.

Second, employers can attempt to access the official criminal records of employees. Even when publicly available, there are various federal regulations regarding fair treatment of the applicant and the requirement that the applicant be notified when a query is made and be given the chance to rectify any mistakes on the criminal history record. For these reasons, employers often turn to private screening firms to perform background checks. The most thorough background checks search county records in all counties of residence for the individual in question in addition to accessing the federal III index. The county-level search may generate information not included in the III data system, especially for arrests for less serious crimes. A 2006 report by the U.S. attorney general estimates that half of arrests in state repositories do not have information on eventual dispositions (U.S. Department of Justice 2006). Arrests for incidents where charges are eventually dropped, or where the individual is convicted of a misdemeanor or felony not resulting in a prison spell (prison terms are recorded on rap sheets) often do not have complete disposition outcomes. For employers who cannot access the III data system, many private background check firms run queries against privately collected databases usually consisting of data sets purchased from county courts or state repositories.

Finally, employers may simply guess based on demeanor, personal presentation, signals on one's resume regarding unexplained absences from the labor market, or in some instances race. Holzer,

Raphael, and Stoll (2006a) find that employers who state an extreme reluctance to hiring ex-offenders and who do not use formal background checks are the least likely to hire African American males. This finding is consistent with employers using race and gender as a simple tool for screening out ex-offenders. Of course, such a screen is likely to be inaccurate in many instances, resulting in discrimination against black males who do not have criminal convictions. It can also lead employers to exclude from consideration black males with criminal histories who may make fine employees, and fail to detect white male applicants and other applicants with criminal histories who may not.

Existing employer surveys suggest widespread use of criminal background checks in screening and hiring. In the California survey discussed earlier, roughly 60 percent of employers indicated that they always check the criminal backgrounds of applicants, while 28 percent indicated that they sometimes check. In a more recent 2009 survey, the Society for Human Resource Management estimates that 93 percent of its member organizations use some form of criminal background screening.[3] While the survey is likely less representative of employers (and more importantly, job openings) than the California survey, both surveys indicate that the vast majority of employers engage in some form of criminal background screening.

To be sure, employers are not free to engage in blanket discrimination against job applicants with criminal histories, though some of the research on this topic that we will discuss in the next section suggests that in some instances this does occur. In 2012, the EEOC issued an enforcement guidance document on the topic, providing direction for employers who use criminal history records on how to screen within the bounds of federal law (EEOC 2012). In light of racial differences in the prevalence of criminal histories and the EEOC's charge to combat discrimination based on race, color, religion, sex, or national origin, the guidance identifies two variations of screening practices that would clearly be in violation and come under the purview of the EEOC. First, selectively using criminal history records in a manner that disadvantages protected groups, such as African American applicants, is unacceptable. Hence, an employer willing to give white former inmates a second chance but who does not extend the same break to black former inmates could be held liable for employment discrimination.

Second, a neutrally applied screen that has a disparate impact on a protected group and is not demonstrably related to the ability of the applicant to perform the job at hand is interpreted by the EEOC as grounds for a discrimination lawsuit. In other words, disparate impact alone is not sufficient to establish a discriminatory impact. It must also be shown that the employment screen creating the disparate impact cannot be validated, in that it does not screen out unsuitable job candidates. The EEOC offers several methods for validating employment screens. The first simply involves a judicious and discerning assessment on a case-by-case basis of applicant criminal histories. The commission recommends that employers make a reasonable effort to consider the nature of the offense, the time that has passed, and the relation of the offense to the current job on an applicant-by-applicant basis. Alternatively, employers can commission research or cite existing social science/criminological research supporting the use of a specific screen to predict applicant suitability. Conversely, plaintiffs seeking remedy for discrimination experienced in the workforce could offer as evidence social science research supporting the contention that the employee's criminal history is irrelevant.

A particularly interesting case cited in the EEOC guidance that has recently spurred new research on this topic is the case of *El v. Southeastern Pennsylvania Transportation Authority* (2007). The plaintiff in the case was a 55-year-old African American man dismissed from his job when his employer learned of a homicide conviction resulting from a gang fight when he was 15 years old. While on appeal, the U.S. Third Circuit Court of Appeals affirmed the summary judgment for the employer. The decision noted that had the plaintiff produced expert testimony demonstrating that the criminal-offending risk of ex-offenders declines to the levels of the average person with sufficient time, the decision may have changed. Interestingly, since the 2007 decision, researchers have turned their attention to this issue. Using various methodological strategies, several researchers have found that within 5 to 10 years of release from prison, the risk of reoffending for those who have desisted from crime drops to the risk level of the average adult (see, for example, Blumstein and Nakamura [2009]). We will discuss this issue in greater depth in Chapter 6.

To summarize, the use of criminal background screening is now widespread in the United States. Employers are increasingly accessing official records through third-party private screening firms that may use multiple means to prepare such background searches. They are not free to blanket discriminate against applicants with criminal history records. Most notably, given the racially disproportionate composition of the population of former prison inmate and ex-offenders, employers who engage in such blanket exclusion run the risk of violating civil rights law.

HIRING OUTCOMES AND EMPLOYMENT PROSPECTS

Certainly there are employers who will not hire former inmates. As we have already discussed, some employers are legally prohibited from doing so. The extreme stated reluctance to hire those with criminal histories likely translates into fewer job offers for job seekers with a documented criminal past.

Sociologist Devah Pager (2003, 2007) provides perhaps the strongest evidence of such an effect. Pager carried out what is referred to as an audit study to assess the role of having served time on the likelihood of being called back for a job interview. Specifically, the audit study employed two pairs of auditors, one pair consisting of two young African American men and the other pair consisting of two young white men. Within each pair, the auditors were chosen to resemble one another in stature, presentation, age, race, gender, and general demeanor. Fictitious resumes were created for each to generate similar levels of work experience and education. The auditors differed with respect to one characteristic. One auditor signaled having been in prison while the other auditor did not. The pairs were then sent out to apply for job openings within the Milwaukee area culled from various sources.

The results of this exercise revealed strong negative effects of time in prison on the likelihood of being called back for an interview. Among the white auditors, 17 percent of those indicating that they had done time were called back compared to 34 percent among those that had not. Among the black auditors, 5 percent of those reporting previous prison time were called back, compared with 14 percent for those who had not. The results suggest that the penalty for having a prison spell in one's past is particularly severe for African Americans. However, the results also indicate that African American men without criminal histories face much poorer odds in the job market. Most saliently, the African American applicants without a criminal history had a lower call-back rate than the white applicants with a criminal history.

Pager, Western, and Bonikowski (2009) confirmed this latter finding with a further audit study carried out in New York City. In this analysis, the authors used two groups of auditors, both of which contained a white, black, and Latino auditor. In the first group, none of the auditors signaled having a criminal record; in the second group, the white auditor signaled having a criminal record while the Latino and black auditor did not. In both instances, the authors discovered higher call-back rates for the white auditor. However, when the white auditor signaled a criminal record, call back rates were lower for all applicants regardless of race.

Several researchers have attempted to test more generally for an adverse effect of having served time on one's employment prospects by analyzing longitudinal data that follow the same people across multiple years. Western (2002) compares the earnings trajectories of a cohort of youth who were 14–22 years of age in 1979. He compares youth who serve time to high-risk youth who do not and finds a sizable relative decline in the hourly wages of the formerly incarcerated. In previous research analyzing the same data set (Raphael 2007), I compare the employment outcomes of youth who serve time early in their lives to those who serve time later in life. I find a significant and substantial negative effect of prior incarceration on annual weeks worked that corresponds in time with one's first incarceration spell.

Using more recent longitudinal data for the United States and a large number of observable personal characteristics, Apel and Sweeten (2010) estimate the effects of a prior incarceration spell on various employment, educational, and criminal justice outcomes after matching youth who serve time to those who don't. The authors find sizable effects of a previous incarceration on the probability of employment five years following. The authors also find some evidence that a prior incarceration predicts future criminal activity and poorer educational outcomes.

A number of studies have used administrative data on arrest and incarceration matched to administrative earnings records collected from employers by the state for the purpose of administering the state unemployment insurance system. Waldfogel (1994) and Grogger (1995) are among the first to pursue this research strategy. Waldfogel uses data on people who are convicted in federal court and compares pre- and postconviction employment outcomes culled from federal parole records. He finds the largest earnings penalties for those who serve time and those convicted of a "breach" crime. Grogger uses California administrative data to study contemporaneous and time-delayed effects of arrest, conviction, probation, being sentenced to jail, and being sentenced to prison on subsequent earnings and employment. He finds that an arrest has a short-lived negative effect on earnings, while serving a prison sentence has a more pronounced and longer-lasting negative effect on earnings.

There are a number of studies that use state and federal prison administrative records combined with state unemployment-insurance earnings records to analyze the pre- and postincarceration employment and earnings patterns of prison inmates. Kling (2006) analyzes data for federal prisoners in California and state prisoners in Florida; Jung (2011) and Cho and Lalonde (2008) examine data for state prisoners in Illinois; Pettit and Lyons (2007) use data for prisoners in Washington State; and Sabol (2007) analyzes data for prisoners in Ohio. While these studies differ from one another along a number of dimensions, there are several consistent findings. First, the unemployment insurance records measure very low employment and earnings among state-prison inmates prior to incarceration (with roughly one-third showing positive quarterly earnings in any given quarter for the two-year period preceding incarceration). While this is partially explained by the incompleteness of administrative data, these findings also suggest low labor force participation rates among soon-to-be inmates.[4]

Second, nearly all of the studies find that employment increases above preincarceration levels immediately following release and then declines to preincarceration levels or falls below preincarceration levels within a couple of years. The small postrelease employment increase is likely driven by the fact that most released prisoners are conditionally released to parole authorities and must meet certain obligations, including employment search or even formal employment requirements (perhaps entailing jobs more likely to be captured in unemployment insurance records), to remain in the community.

A final group of studies uses data from the U.S. census to estimate the relationship between the proportion of a given demographic that is incarcerated and the average employment outcomes of the non-incarcerated among the corresponding group (Raphael 2006, 2011). These studies show that the demographic subgroups that experience the largest increase in incarceration rates also experience the largest decreases in employment among the nonincarcerated.

To summarize, the existing research tends to find substantial adverse effects of involvement with the criminal justice system on employment and earnings prospects. Audit studies show much lower call-back rates among job applicants who signal a criminal history. Longitudinal studies that compare earnings and employment trajectories of those who serve time to those who do not find relatively poor labor market performance among those with criminal histories. Finally, we observe large declines in employment rates since the 1970s among groups who have experienced the largest increases in incarceration rates.

IMPLICATIONS FOR THE U.S. LABOR MARKET

Due in large part to the increase in U.S. incarceration rates, employers increasingly screen the criminal histories of their applicants and make hiring decisions accordingly. Employers arguably have good reason to consider such histories and have increasing accessibility to such information through third-party intermediaries that specialize in background checks. This practice has come under the scrutiny of the EEOC given the likely disparate impact that criminal background screening has on the employment prospects of minority job applicants.

Ample empirical evidence exists regarding employers' extreme reluctance to hire former prisoners and others with criminal convictions. Moreover, existing empirical research documents adverse effects of doing time on long-term employment prospects. Given the increase in U.S. incarceration rates documented in Chapter 2 and the disparate impact of this increase, it is likely the case that substantial proportions of minority males, African American males in particular, face increasingly circumscribed labor markets where attaining employment with many employers is simply not possible.

This is a challenging set of circumstances facing individuals leaving prison and the service providers that aim to ease this reentry. Chapter 5 discusses what we know from evaluation research regarding the efficacy of employment based reentry efforts.

Notes

1. See the Federal Bonding Web site: http://bonds4jobs.com/ (accessed November 6, 2013).
2. Roughly one-quarter of the employers in the California survey indicated that they were legally proscribed from hiring certain ex-offenders (see Raphael [2011]).
3. See the Society for Human Resource Management Web site: http://www .slideshare.net/shrm/background-check-criminal (accessed on June 25, 2013).
4. Kling (2006) is the only study that compares employment as measured by quarterly earnings records to inmate self-reported employment at the time of arrest. He reports that while only 33 percent of inmates have positive earnings in the typical preincarceration quarter, nearly 65 percent report being employed at the time of arrest. Based on analysis of Current Population Survey data for comparable men, Kling concludes that most of this disparity reflects the fact that inmates are employed in informal jobs where employers are not paying social security taxes or paying into the Unemployment Insurance system.

Chapter 5

Employment-Based
Prisoner Reentry Programs

Do We Know What Works?

With the tremendous increase in U.S. incarceration rates and the consequent increase in the annual outflow of prison inmates, reentry services are receiving greater attention from researchers and policymakers. An increasing minority of U.S. men (and for some demographic subgroups the majority) will at some point face the challenge of reintegrating into noninstitutional society after a spell in prison. Identifying effective practices for fostering success in reentry is of paramount importance.

Since the passage of the 2007 Second Chance Act, the federal government has distributed, on average, roughly $65 million per year to states and localities that provide reentry services for recently released inmates. Aside from these federal funds, parole officers, probation officers, social service departments, hospitals, and in some instances public housing authorities help to address the reentry needs of former prisoners. To be sure, the cost burdens of reentry are certainly born to a great degree by the families of former prison inmates. Many inmates return to families for shelter and sustenance. Because many former inmates, especially those coming off very long prison spells, face an unusually high risk of homelessness upon release, it is undoubtedly the case that the families of former inmates privately bear many reentry costs.

There are several objectives of reentry programs, the first and perhaps most important of which is to keep former inmates from returning to prison. The rearrest rate of former prison inmates is quite high—roughly two-thirds will be rearrested within three years, and one-quarter are sent back to prison (Langan and Levin 2002). Recidivism is costly in terms of both direct public outlays and new criminal victimizations.

Second, reentry programs aim to minimize the degree of material poverty experienced by recently released prison inmates. Most inmates are poor going into prison and poorer coming out. Their assets often do not extend beyond the minimal amount of "gate money" (usually no more than a couple hundred dollars) given to them by corrections authorities upon release. Many have weakened and strained ties with family members and face a high risk of homelessness. Reentry service providers devote considerable effort to basic physical needs and logistics, such as procuring identification, evaluating public benefits eligibility, and finding suitable shelter.

Third, reentry programs aim to help former inmates assume positive and conventional roles and responsibilities, including reuniting with family, supporting dependents, abiding by the law, and desisting from self-destructive activity such as drug abuse.

Naturally, obtaining and maintaining employment is central to achieving these objectives. Most released inmates are males of primary working age, a period of life when social expectations are that one will be a gainfully employed, contributing member of society. Conventional wisdom holds that employment is central to criminal desistance, although the research reviewed below suggests that this link isn't as strong as one would think. However, employment is certainly central to avoiding poverty, avoiding acute income crises, and to effectively assuming adult responsibilities interrupted by one's spell in prison. In this chapter, I review what we know about income support and employment-based efforts to aid the reentry of convicted criminal offenders into noninstitutional society.

EXPERIMENTAL VERSUS NONEXPERIMENTAL
EVALUATIONS OF PRISONER REENTRY PROGRAMS

Given the fractious nature of corrections in the United States (there are 51 independent corrections systems), there are a multitude of programs designed to aid reentry of released prison inmates or minimize criminal activity through the delivery of various services.[1] In many instances these programs are sanctioned and funded by state governments and coordinate service delivery with state parole and local probation departments. Many such programs also receive funding from various federal government agencies and in some instances private foundations.

As there is no standard set of reentry services delivered across the country, there are literally hundreds of alternative programs and approaches ranging from cognitive behavioral therapy to family reunification services to employment services of all forms for released inmates and high-risk individuals. Consequently, there are also hundreds of empirical evaluations of these efforts.

Among social scientists who engage in empirical research, there is a strong distinction drawn between experimental—or, in the language of evaluators, randomized-control trial and nonexperimental evaluations. The distinction between the two is worth noting, as most program evaluation research on prisoner reentry programs involves nonexperimental evaluations that are often interpreted with caution for reasons to be discussed shortly.

Simply put, experimental evaluations first identify a target population of study subjects and then randomly assign the subjects to either a treatment group or a control group. The treatment group receives the intervention while the control group does not. By monitoring the outcome of interest over time, the effect of a programmatic intervention can be measured by comparing posttreatment outcomes among the treatment group and the control group. Any difference in outcomes is attributable to the program. Randomization ensures that members of the treatment group on average will be similar to members of the control group and that those who are particularly motivated or stand the most to gain from program participation are not overrepresented among those receiving treatment.

By contrast, nonexperimental evaluations compare outcomes of those who participate in a program to those who do not without controlling the process by which individuals select into participation. Absent researcher control over who participates, it is always possible that some unobservable factor may explain away an apparent impact of the treatment on program participants. For example, successful criminal desistance among those participating in a job training program relative to those who do not observed in a nonexperimental setting may be attributable to average differences in motivation between participants and nonparticipants that are difficult to quantify and control for. Not surprisingly, nonexperimental evaluations of programs designed to help former prison inmates tend to find much larger effects than experimental evaluations.

To be sure, there have been great advances in nonexperimental research techniques designed to make treatment and comparison groups as alike as possible with the aim of statistically isolating the effect of program interventions on social outcomes. However, there are methodological problems associated with experimental evaluations—problems that often tip the balance for researchers and evaluators toward nonexperimental research methods. For example, it is likely the case that program interventions vary in their efficaciousness across participants. Clearly, those who stand to benefit the most from receiving reentry services following release from prison should be the most likely to seek out such services. Whether or not one is randomized into the treatment group of a specific program does not preclude those who would benefit the most from seeking out services elsewhere, especially when there are many small competing service providers. To the extent that this occurs, the results from an experimental research design will be compromised.

A related issue concerns the fact that those induced to participate through randomization are likely individuals who benefit the least from the program. For example, suppose there are two types of released inmates: those who are very motivated and who benefit greatly from job search assistance, and those who are relatively unmotivated and who benefit but not as much. In a world with multiple service providers, the motivated will always seek out and find services, while the unmotivated may or may not. An experimental evaluation that randomly assigns potential recipients of job search assistance will have an impact on program participation only among the unmotivated. Consequently, the program effect estimates from such an evaluation will basically measure the impact for the group that stands to benefit the least, and miss the large effects on employment for the motivated participants who always participate. These caveats aside, most researchers consider evaluations conducted in randomized-control settings to be of higher quality and generally subject nonexperimental evaluations to higher levels of scrutiny.

Nearly all evaluations of prisoner reentry programs are nonexperimental. In their exhaustive meta-analysis of all English-language evaluations of prisoner reentry and crime-abatement programs, Drake, Aos, and Miller (2009) identify 545 such program evaluations. Less than 5 percent of these evaluations utilize a randomized-control research design. The authors searched for all English language evaluations conducted since the 1970s that met three broad criteria: 1) each evaluation had to make use of a comparison sample where the treatment and comparison groups were relatively similar on average, 2) evaluations had to include program dropouts as well as program completers when assessing the effect of a program intervention, and 3) the evaluation must contain estimates for an impact of some indicator of criminal activity, be it self-reported, arrest, or conviction. Using all available evaluations that meet these criteria, Drake, Aos, and Miller estimate the average impact on the criminal outcome for over 50 prototypical in-prison and postprison interventions.[2]

The meta-analysis yields fairly large average effects of in-prison vocational and basic education programs (on the order of 9 percent reductions in criminal activity among the treated).[3] Drake, Aos, and Miller (2009) also find an impact of roughly 7 percent of in-prison cognitive behavioral therapy. Such therapy focuses on the thoughts, assumptions, and beliefs of the criminally active, with the aim of identifying thought patterns leading to negative behaviors and imparting participants with the tools for correcting these thought processes (National Research Council 2007). Postrelease workforce development efforts are also found to reduce criminal offending by roughly 5 percent. Moreover, basic drug treatment programs during incarceration as well as following release yield benefits in terms of reduced crime that tend to outweigh costs, although the National Research Council (2007) finds that jail-based drug treatment programs (as opposed to programs delivered while in prison) appear to be ineffective on average.

The meta-analysis provides a good starting point for framing the scope of prisoner reentry efforts in the United States, and the work is frequently cited and consulted by state corrections authorities across the country aiming to identify cost-effective reentry programs. However, keeping in mind the vastness of the body of nonexperimental evaluations and the great variation in evaluation quality, I now turn to a discussion of what we have learned from social experiments aimed at increasing the employability and reducing the criminality of former inmates.

RESULTS FROM EXPERIMENTAL EVALUATIONS OF EMPLOYMENT-BASED PROGRAMS

Over the past three decades, there have been a handful of experimental evaluations of programs that are intended to reduce criminal activity and foster employment among either former inmates or high-risk groups. The meta-analysis by Visher, Winterfield, and Coggeshall

(2005) identifies all such experimental evaluations occurring in the United States through the late 1990s. Here I review the results of this research along with findings from more recent experimental studies of prisoner reentry efforts.

There have been several evaluations that assess whether income support for released inmates reduces recidivism rates. The Living Insurance for Ex-Prisoners (LIFE) program was carried out in Baltimore between 1972 and 1974 (Maller and Thornton 1978; Rossi, Berk, and Lenihan 1980). The target population was former inmates with a very high likelihood of future arrest for a property crime and no history of drug or alcohol dependence returning from prison to the Baltimore area. The program defined four treatment groups. The first group received a $60 check once a week for 13 weeks, along with job placement assistance. The program design called for benefits to decline with increases in labor income, but in practice all men received the full amount of their grant within 13 weeks or shortly thereafter. The second group received financial assistance but no job placement services. The third group received unlimited job placement services only. The final was a control group receiving nothing.

Among those receiving financial assistance, arrests for property crimes were 8.3 percentage points lower, and the proportion not arrested over the subsequent year was 7.4 percentage points higher. There was no statistically significant effect of treatment on employment, where the presumption was that the program created very large negative incentives against working (see Chapter 2 of Rossi, Berk, and Lenihan [1980]). There were also no measurable benefits from receiving job placement assistance.[4]

Based on these findings, the Temporary Aid Research Project (TARP) implemented an income-support program on a larger scale (Rossi, Berk, and Lenihan 1980). A key difference relative to the LIFE program, however, was that the program was administered through the state agencies handling unemployment insurance claims. This was meant to mimic how such a program would actually operate if brought to scale by a specific state. In addition, treatment groups were defined to create variation in length of benefits as well as benefit reduction rates, and the programs were implemented in different states (Georgia and Texas). The TARP program contained five randomized treatment groups. Three of the groups received financial assistance (one for 26 weeks with benefits reduced dollar-for-dollar with labor earnings, one for 13 weeks also with a dollar-for-dollar benefit reduction rate, and one for 13 weeks where benefits were reduced by 25 cents for each dollar of labor earnings) with the provision that unused allotment at the end of the specified period could be used for a period of up to a year. A fourth group was offered employment services only, a fifth group was offered nothing but payment for the interviews, and a sixth group was also identified that was not interviewed but for whom administrative records were analyzed.

The evaluators found no effect of the intervention on arrests, either overall or for specific crimes, in either state. However, there were substantial negative impacts of the program on employment. The authors speculate that the lack of an impact on arrests reflects offsetting impact on criminal activity of the decline in employment (leading to more criminal activity) and the transition aid leading to less criminal activity.

A number of studies have evaluated the impact of providing transitional jobs on the employment and criminal activity of high-risk populations. The National Supported Work (NSW) intervention, implemented during the 1970s, targeted four hard-to-employ groups: 1) long-term welfare recipients (those receiving Aid to Families With Dependent Children [AFDC] benefits); 2) ex-offenders defined as those convicted and incarcerated for a crime in the last six months; 3) drug-addicts defined as those currently enrolled in a drug treatment program; and 4) high school dropouts (Manpower Development Research Corporation [MDRC] 1980). While the original evaluation distinguished drug addicts from ex-offenders, it is likely the case that there was a fair degree of overlap among these groups. Ninety percent of the ex-addicts had prior arrests, with the average participants having served nontrivial amounts of time. The selection criteria were chosen to ensure selection of the most disadvantaged in terms of labor market prospects. Regarding ex-offenders, the eligibility criteria were "age 18 or older; incarcerated within the last six months as the result of a conviction." For ex-addicts, the criteria were "age 18 or older; enrolled in a drug treatment program currently or within the preceding six months."

The NSW program provided transitional jobs in work crews with "graduated stress" in terms of productivity and punctuality requirements as time on the program increased. Participants were time limited in terms of how long they could remain employed in the transitional job, with the limits varying across sites from 12 to 18 months. The impacts differed substantially by participant type. The long-term AFDC recipients experienced significant increases in employment after leaving their supported-work jobs. To be specific, by the last quarter of the follow-up period (25–27 months after enrollment), quarterly employment rates for AFDC treatment members exceeded that of the control group by 7.1 percentage points. By that point, none of the treatment group members were employed in a transitional supported-work job. They also experienced significant increases in earnings and wages and significant decreases in welfare benefits.

For former addicts, there was a delayed impact on post-transitional-jobs employment, with significant and substantial increases (on the order of 10 percentage points) in employment up to two years after leaving the program. In a series of comparisons of cumulative arrests and convictions following random assignment, the researchers find significant impacts on the amount of criminal activity committed by former addicts, with much of the program impact appearing to coincide with being employed. Finally, there was very little evidence of any impact on any outcomes for the ex-offender group.

Christopher Uggen (2000) reanalyzes the data from the NSW demonstration with an explicit focus on how the effectiveness of the program varied by age. Unlike the initial evaluation, Uggen pools all respondents with a prior criminal history and analyzes the impact of being assigned to placement in a transitional job on the arrest rate and the likelihood of earning illegal income. After stratifying the treatment groups into those aged 26 and under and those aged 27 and over, Uggen finds no treatment effect for the younger group but quite large effects on arrests for the older group (on the order of 10 percentage points on the cumulative arrest probability by the end of three years).

Redcross et al. (2012) conducted a more recent evaluation of a program in New York City—offered by the Center for Employment Opportunities (CEO)—which provides transitional employment to former inmates, along with basic educational services (when needed), job training that focuses on soft skills, and other forms of social support. Program participants work in crews and perform services for various public and private sector clients. The program was subject to a rigorous randomized control evaluation by researchers at MDRC for a cohort of participants entering the program in 2004 and 2005. Participation among those assigned to the treatment group was high (roughly 70 percent), and the typical participant remained in a transitional job for about 18 weeks. Once a participant demonstrated stability and solid work skills, a CEO staff member facilitated the transition to a regular employer.

The evaluations of this program show large employment effects for the first three quarters following random assignment that are entirely due to a high propensity to be employed in CEO-provided transitional jobs in the treatment group. By the fourth quarter following assignment, however, the difference in employment rates between the treatment and control groups disappears. Over the course of the full three-year evaluations, the research team found little evidence that the CEO program increased employment in nonsubsidized jobs.

Regarding recidivism, the evaluation demonstrated fairly large reductions in various gauges of future criminal activity, especially among program participants recently released from prison. Over the full three-year follow-up period, the percentage of treatment group members reconvicted was 5.6 percentage points lower than the percentage of control group members reconvicted (a reduction of 11 percent relative to the control group). Consequently, subsequent incarceration levels were also lower among those randomly assigned to the treatment group. Interestingly, this effect is concentrated among those participants who began CEO within three months of release from prison. For this group, the difference in reconviction rates between treatment and control group members was 10 percentage points (a 17 percent reduction relative to the reconviction level of control group members). Among study subjects who came to CEO more than three months after leaving prison, there was no measurable differences between treatment and control group members in recidivism outcomes.

This pattern is consistent with the time-profile of the likelihood of failing on parole following release from prison. It is a well-known and well-documented fact that the likelihood that a person released from prison is returned to custody is highest in the first few months following release and then declines quite sharply thereafter (National Research Council 2008). The findings above are consistent with CEO having the largest impacts for those in the midst of this high-risk period. Conversely, a program targeted at individuals who have survived the high-hazard period may not yield as large an impact as an intervention targeted at those who have just been released.

MDRC's cost-benefit analysis of the CEO program clearly shows that the program generates benefits in excess of costs, and may lead to the conclusion that transitional jobs is clearly the way to go. However, a concurrent evaluation of the Transitional Jobs Reentry Demonstration (TJRD) yields much more disappointing results. The TJRD was implemented in four Midwestern cities: Chicago, Detroit, Milwaukee, and St. Paul. At each site, recently released prison inmates were randomly assigned to either a treatment group that received job search counseling and transitional jobs or a control group that received job search assistance only. Study sites varied in terms of the service providers implementing the program, whether both service components (the job search assistance component and the transitional jobs component) were administered by the same organization or difference organization, and whether employment retention bonuses were available for treatment group members that transitioned into unsubsidized employment. However, the basic structure of what was offered to treatment group and control group members was similar.

Jacobs (2012) conducted the empirical evaluation of this effort. Similar to the results from the CEO evaluation, the TJRD treatment group members experienced a large increase in employment for the first few quarters following random assignment. This increase was entirely due to being offered a transitional job. In fact, there is some evidence that the transitional employment offer reduced the likelihood that program participants found unsubsidized jobs. This employment boost, however, disappears after a few quarters and there is no measurable long-term impact on employment.

The real departure relative to the CEO evaluation concerns recidivism. The evaluation finds no evidence of an effect of transitional jobs in these four cites on any measure of future criminal activity. This is a particularly striking contrast as the study subjects were all offered treatment within three months of being released from prison, the group for which the CEO evaluation found the largest impacts on recidivism.

It's difficult to divine from the two evaluations why the CEO was effective and the TJRD was not. One possibility concerns the fact that in several TJRD sites different organizations were in charge of the transitional jobs component and the employment service component. The CEO has a well-integrated program where job counselors develop close relationships with program participants through the training, transitional jobs, and job placement processes. Perhaps a more balkanized program loses this cohesive element. While the results were not significant, it is notable that there are hints of recidivism effects at the Chicago site, where the entire program was run by the Safer Foundation, a group devoted to reentry services for former inmates. Perhaps a larger sample size would have detected impacts similar to those observed for CEO.

An alternative possibility raised by the authors of the CEO evaluation concerns the use of work crews by CEO. Redcross et al. (2012)

speculate that perhaps the opportunity to interact with other recently released inmates in a positive environment may have altered perception and attitudes toward work for the better. The juxtaposed evaluation of relatively similar intervention suggests that with regard to transitional jobs programs, the jury is still out. The CEO evaluation is certainly a bright spot on the reentry landscape. However, the disappointing results from the TJRD evaluation suggest that the implementation details must matter and that further research is needed.

A number of programs have been targeted at what one might consider high-risk individuals who may have already offended and done time or who have a high likelihood of offending. Some of these efforts were not specifically designed to reduce recidivism or the likelihood of participation in criminal activity, yet they treated many individuals who would be the target recipients of such efforts. For example, out-of-school youth were among the groups targeted by the national Job Training Partnership Act (JTPA) evaluation (Bloom et al. 1994).

The evaluation used a randomized-control design to evaluate the labor market impacts of the workforce development services offered under JTPA. The evaluation randomized eligible program applicants to either a treatment or control group at a nonrandom set of 16 service delivery areas between 1987 and 1989. For all participants, the impact of treatment on earnings and employment were estimated for the two-and-a-half years following randomization.[5] The study looked specifically at four target groups: adult men, adult women, and out-of-school-youth of each gender. For out-of-school youth, the evaluation also assessed the impact of the program on self-reported arrest.

The JTPA program involves what one might consider traditional workforce development programs: on-the-job training, job-search assistance, remedial classroom instruction, and occupational training. It significantly increased completion of the General Educational Development (GED) test among high school dropouts (over 10 percentage point effects for adult high school dropouts) and had substantial effects on earnings for adult males and females (on the order of

8–15 percent). There were no effects of the intervention on the earnings and employment of disadvantaged youth of either gender.

The analysis of arrest outcomes for youth was based on self-reports. Among those youth with prior arrests, there was no measurable impact of treatment on arrest. Among male youth who had never been arrested, there was a significant increase in arrests observed for treatment group members (on the order of 5–7 percentage points). Bloom et al. (1994) speculate that this might be the result of the fact that the JTPA program encouraged participants to be forthright about their involvement with the criminal justice system with employers.

The Job Corps program, which targets disadvantaged youth aged 16–24, provides a much more intensive intervention. Most participants in the program (usually over 80 percent) reside at a Job Corps center, with the average participant staying eight months. Treatment involves a heavy dose of academics, vocational training, and life skills courses. Schochet, Burghardt, and Glazerman (2001) conducted an evaluation of the program, which randomized a subset of the more than 80,000 Job Corps applicants from 1994 to 1996 to either a control group (that was prohibited from enrolling in Job Corps for four years) or a treatment group that was offered a spot. Roughly 73 percent of the treatment group members took up services. A small portion (around 3 percent) of the control group crossed over (mostly three years postrandomization).

The program had substantial effects on educational attainment and vocational training. Treatment group members completed the equivalent of an additional year of schooling relative to control group members. Given the relationship between educational attainment and offending documented in Lochner and Moretti (2004), this particular aspect of the Job Corps program may explain the factors behind the observed treatment effect on offending. The program also had sizable effects on employment (on the order of 5 percentage points) and earnings for the period starting roughly one year after randomization (most participants left the program within a year of starting). During the first four quarters after randomization, the arrest rate for the treatment group was roughly 1 percentage point lower relative to the control group (relative to control base of 3–5 percent). These arrest effects are highly significant. There was a 3 percentage point difference in the proportion convicted over the 48 postrandomization months and a 2 percentage point difference in the proportion incarcerated. These effect sizes are relative to control baselines of 25.2 and 17.9 percent, respectively. Estimated impacts were substantially larger for men. The arrest treatment effect was 5 percentage points, the convicted treatment effect was 4 percentage points, and the incarcerated treatment effect was 3.1 percentage points, all significant at the 5 percent level. There were no significant effects for females or for male nonresidents.

It is noteworthy that in contrast to the JTPA evaluation, Job Corps delivered significant impacts on both employment as well as criminal offending for youth. The large impact on educational attainment may have been one important mediating factor. Clearly, the residential component of the program is likely to have been important as well, as this aspect of the program likely removed youth from social networks that may have enhanced the likelihood of poor outcomes. Despite the high costs associated with this program, it is notable that cost-benefit analysis accompanying the official evaluation concludes that Job Corps passes the cost-benefit test. Most of the benefits occur in the form of the value of increased productivity as well as a reduction in service use among program participants (McConnell and Glazerman 2001).

The JOBSTART program is largely patterned after the Job Corps program, the key differences being that JOBSTART does not provide a stipend and is a nonresidential program (Cave et al. 1993). The program targets 17–21-year-old high school dropouts and delivers academic services, occupational and vocational training, and job placement services. The randomized-control evaluation of this program was principally concerned with the domains of educational attainment and employment outcomes, though it also includes information on welfare receipts, fertility, and criminal activity (based on whether one is ever arrested). There is no information on incarceration.

Similar to the results for Job Corps, JOBSTART had a large treatment effect on the likelihood of completing a GED or a high school diploma (on the order of 13 percentage points). Treatment group members experienced small declines in employment and earnings in the first postrandomization year (most likely due to the time demands of participation in the program), and slightly higher earnings and employment in all other years. With regard to arrests, the treatment had a fairly large impact on the likelihood of being arrested in the first year for male participants (over 6 percentage points), but no impact on the arrest likelihood at the end of the four-year evaluation.

A final program evaluation targeting at-risk youth is the National Guard Youth ChalleNGe program (Millenky et al. 2011). This program aims to help youth who have dropped out of school. It starts with a 2-week physically grueling intake experience, followed by a 20-week residential program, and a year nonresidential mentoring program. The intervention emphasizes military-style discipline, completion of a GED, and basic life skills training. The program does not accept those with criminal histories other than youth with arrests for juvenile status offenses.[6] In light of the fact that most who end up in prison commit crimes and are arrested at very young ages, the youth targeted by this intervention may be somewhat less at risk for future criminality than youth who will eventually serve prison time. While the program was ongoing, a randomized-control evaluation was performed by MDRC.

Over the three-year follow-up period, MDRC evaluators found that of those assigned to treatment, there were large increases in the proportion that completed a GED, earned some college credits, and boosted their earnings, and there was a greater likelihood of this group being employed. There were also substantial and statistically significant differences in the amount of idle time, with members of the treatment group much more likely to be engaged in productive activity. Although the three-year evaluation found no significant differences between treatment and control group members in the proportion ever arrested or convicted of a crime, earlier evaluations roughly one year and two years following random assignment found discretely lower arrests among treatment group members. The final evaluation did not analyze the impact on total arrests or whether one had done time, but it may certainly be the case that having been arrested later on average than members of the control group actually reflects lower overall levels of criminal activity over the entire three-year period.

IMPLICATIONS FOR THE EMPLOYMENT OF FORMER PRISONERS

To summarize the results from past evaluations, there is some evidence that income support, transitional employment, and human capital investments in former and potential future inmates may reduce criminal behavior and recidivism. The results, however, are not entirely consistent across studies. Perhaps the weakest evidence is observed for income support. There is reason to believe that the small-scale intervention under the LIFE program involved very intensive case work among program implementers on behalf of the former inmates, while delivery of income support through the TARP program occurred at arm's length and involved much more rigorous enforcement of the benefit reductions with labor income. Any large-scale implementation of such assistance is perhaps more likely to take the form of the TARP evaluation than the LIFE program, calling into question this approach. Nonetheless, these are the only two experimental studies exploring the effects of income support. Such efforts combined with different sets of services or alternative rules regarding interactions with labor income may yield different outcomes.

Transitional employment appears to have promise, though this conclusion is tempered somewhat by the TJRD evaluation. Both the NSW and CEO evaluations find substantial evidence of heterogeneity in program effect, suggesting that perhaps the hardest to serve are the least likely to benefit. It is somewhat surprising that despite large

impacts on employment in the first few quarters following assignment, the CEO evaluation finds little overall impact on measures of
criminal offending. While this may be due to the sampling frame used
to generate experimental subjects, this basic pattern for year one is
sobering.

Perhaps the brightest prospects are observed for at-risk youth programs. All of the programs reviewed (JTPA, Job Corps, JOBSTART,
ChalleNGe) have substantial impacts on the educational attainment of
participants, with Job Corps adding nearly a full year of instructional
time. The more extensive measures of criminal behavior in Job Corps
and JOBSTART both yielded evidence of substantial impacts of these
programs on criminal participation. The diminished effects by year
three for ChalleNGe are disappointing, but the combined evaluations
for this program are likely indicative of less overall offending among
program participants within three years of entry.

The exhaustive review of nonexperimental research provided
by the Washington State Institute of Public Policy does provide support for the cost-effectiveness of several within-prison rehabilitation
efforts, including cognitive behavioral therapy, within prison occupational training, and drug treatment programs. To the extent that such
efforts remediate the basic work and life skill deficiencies commonly
observed among those doing time, such efforts in addition to reducing
recidivism are likely to improve employment prospects.

Many in the prisoner reentry field believe in the importance of
continuity in service provision, which begins with solid reentry planning for inmates before they are released and continues with the drug
treatment and counseling services available within the community.
Unfortunately, many inmates are released with little such planning
and often find themselves without proper identification, without a
place a stay, and with very little money in their pockets. A recent effort
in San Francisco to bridge the transition may provide a more productive model for reentry planning. In a coordinated effort between the
county's sheriff's department and the city's Department of Adult Probation, San Francisco has created a "reentry pod" in the county jail,

whereby inmates to be released to the county within three months are transferred to the jail pod. In the short time before release, probation helps align the soon-to-be released inmate with any services needed and public support programs that the person is eligible for, and helps with basic needs such as procuring identification and making sure the person has somewhere to go after his or her release. While this is a new effort with no evaluation results to date, this is a particularly creative concept that merits watching in the coming months and years.

Notes

1. This section draws heavily from the review of existing programs in Raphael (2011).
2. Drake, Aos, and Miller (2009) developed a five-point scale with higher values indicating a stronger methodological design. A score of five was assigned to randomized-control studies. Studies employing quasi-experimental research designs with good balance on covariates between the treatment and control samples that adjust for observable differences between treatment and comparison observations were assigned a score of four. The authors note that convincing instrumental variables studies, regression-discontinuity studies, as well as natural experiments fall into this grouping. Other rigorous quasi-experimental studies with less convincing identification strategies were assigned a value of three. A two was assigned when pretreatment values for covariates and outcomes are imbalanced between the comparison and treatment groups, while a value of one was assigned to studies that did not employ a comparison group. The authors only include studies with a value of three or higher. In the meta-analysis, effect sizes for group three studies are discounted by 50 percent while effect sizes for group four studies are discounted by 25 percent. Group five effect sizes are not discounted.
3. The gauges of criminal activity vary considerably across the studies included in this meta-analysis, although most are based on post-treatment arrests and convictions. The studies also vary according to the follow-up time periods of analysis. The authors include the estimated impact on the longest follow-up period reported in each study.
4. In a linear probability model of posttreatment arrest, Mallar and Thorton (1978) estimate a marginal effect of job placement assistance of 0.053 with a standard error of 0.0418 in a model controlling for being assigned to receive financial assistance, a quadratic in age, having at least a high school degree, and a dummy indicating white.

5. The then General Accounting Office produced a long-term follow-up study in 1996 that estimated program impacts on earnings and employment for five years posttreatment. Much of the positive effects on earnings and employment for adult men and women were found to disappear over this longer-term period (General Accounting Office 1996).

6. A juvenile status offense is any offense that is a violation solely due to the fact that the individual is a juvenile. Underage drinking, violating curfews, and truancy are the most frequent status offenses.

Chapter 6
Policies for Moving Forward

While former inmates represent a small segment of the U.S. labor market, they are perhaps the most disadvantaged group of job seekers. Although this segment likely includes no more than 7 percent of the adult population, it includes a substantial proportion of low-skilled and minority men and a majority of relatively less-educated African American men. The portrait painted here is bleak. The poorest and least skilled members of the U.S. adult population are increasingly cycling through the U.S. prison system, acquiring criminal history records as well as the social designation of former prisoner, and then trying to survive in the noninstitutionalized world with this stigma. This largely male population is currently employed at historically low rates and is accumulating less formal work experience over the course of their lives than those who do not serve time. These individuals face hurdles created by the personal characteristics that they bring with them into the criminal justice system (low education, little work experience, early criminal activity), as well as their experiences while incarcerated. Moreover, these hurdles are compounded by legitimate concerns among many employers regarding their suitability as employees, as well as outright and unjustified labor market discrimination.

The reentry policy challenge in the United States has grown in tandem with the near fivefold increase in the U.S. incarceration rate. Over 700,000 prison inmates are released each year, each requiring housing, jobs, and a host of social services aimed at reintegrating them into noninstitutionalized society. The centrality of stable employment for these released inmates is without question. While the relationship between recidivism and employment is complicated—placing former inmates in low-wage jobs to prevent future criminal activity is not necessarily the answer—there is ample social science research to suggest that labor market prospects in general influence the likelihood of criminal offending.[1] It is hard to envision productive roles for prime-aged men that do not involve stable and legitimate employment.

As we have discussed, the constellation of reentry services offered to former prison inmates is vast and varying in terms of approach. Many providers focus on the very basics of reintegration, including acquiring proper identification and meeting minimal housing and income needs. Several specialized service providers focus on the specific health and mental health needs that are disproportionately observed among former prison inmates. Others focus on remediating issues that may prevent stable employment and successful reintegration, including poor cognitive processing skills, substance abuse, and basic educational deficits. All of these services are certainly vital, and we are likely underinvesting in these basic human capital development efforts for this well-identified and highly problematic population. We should be devoting more resources to such efforts.

However, it is clear to many that the reentry challenges we face are essentially the product of our own past policy choices. The high incarceration rate in the United States is not the product of a crime wave or offending levels that are out of control relative to other countries—it is the product of a sequence of federal and state legislative acts, passed with regularity and frequency over the last few decades, aimed at getting tough on crime and on convicted criminals.

In this final chapter, I offer some thoughts regarding policy prescriptions that I believe would have a first-order effect on mitigating the U.S. prisoner reentry challenge. While the efforts of reentry service providers are certainly to be applauded and supported, I believe that the core cause of the reentry problem is driven by our inefficient and overuse of prison as a crime control mechanism. Additionally, once inmates are released, policymakers could do more to triage high-risk and low-risk releases and shoulder the uncertainty faced by employers in hiring former inmates, a factor that may counter the stigma associated with a criminal conviction.

SCALING BACK THE USE OF INCARCERATION
AS PUNISHMENT

Since the passage of federal sentencing reforms in the mid to late 1980s, drug offenders apprehended by the federal Drug Enforcement Administration and prosecuted in federal court by U.S. attorneys have faced stiff mandatory minimum sentences and long prison terms in federal penitentiaries. In the years since, the federal prison system has grown eightfold, with roughly half of federal prison inmates serving time for a drug offense. In August 2013, U.S. Attorney General Eric Holder announced a major policy shift in the sentencing of low-level drug offenders in federal courts: drug quantities would no longer be listed in the charge. As a result, prosecutors in federal cases essentially bypass the mandatory minimum sentences, permitting judges more liberty to graduate the sanction according to the severity of the offense.

In a speech to the American Bar Association, Holder cited the significant financial and social costs associated with incarcerating low-level offenders and the need to prioritize in the face of the federal budget sequester.[2] Beyond economic costs, however, Holder noted that many who are serving long sentences pose very little threat to society: "It's clear . . . that too many Americans go to too many prisons for far too long, and for no truly good law enforcement reason. It's clear, at a basic level, that twentieth-century criminal justice solutions are not adequate to overcome our twenty-first-century challenges. And it is well past time to implement common sense changes that will foster safer communities from coast to coast."

Holder's sentiments are supported by a growing body of empirical research suggesting that the crime-fighting effects of incarceration are subject to what economists call diminishing marginal returns. To be specific, prison affects crime rates through two primary avenues. First, by incapacitating someone in an institution, they are physically prevented from committing further crime. Second, the threat of punishment with a prison sentence likely deters crime.[3] Research on this topic tends to suggest that for the most part, prison reduces crime through incapacitation (see Buonanno and Raphael [2013]).

There is ample evidence that prisons incapacitate criminally active people. However, this incapacitation effect varies considerably from inmate to inmate, and for some inmates it is trivially small to nonexistent. This heterogeneity in the propensity to offend among those we incarcerate has increased greatly with the expansion of the prison population, with the average propensity to offend declining. In other words, the average offender incarcerated today is much less criminally prone than the average offender incarcerated in years past. The proportion of offenders with very low probability of reoffending, especially for serious violent crimes, is also higher than in years past.

These patterns are suggestive of diminishing marginal crime-fighting benefits to incarceration. Put simply, the incarceration rate grows when we apply incarceration as punishment more liberally (e.g., in punishing less serious as well as more serious felonies) or when we apply incarceration more intensively (e.g., when we hand out longer sentences). Applying prison sentences more liberally essentially casts a wider net across the population of offenders reining in less serious offenders along with the more serious. Applying incarceration more intensively incarcerates people into advanced ages, when offending levels generally fall. Interestingly, even among prison inmates, there is a strong decline in within-prison offending with age (Raphael and Stoll 2013, Chapter 7). Both dimensions of expansion imply that the bang-per-buck spent on prisons in terms of crimes prevented will be lower when incarceration rates are high.

Several researchers have documented diminishing crime-fighting benefits to prison in the United States, with most showing that the amount of crime prevented per prison years served is currently quite low and skewed toward less serious crimes (see Johnson and Raphael 2012; Liedka, Piehl, and Useem 2006; Owens 2009; and Raphael and Stoll 2013). Others have demonstrated diminishing returns in other countries with much lower incarceration rates than the United States.

(Buonanno and Raphael [2013] provide evidence for Italy; Vollaard [2013] provides evidence for the Netherlands.) Moreover, there is ample empirical research supporting the efficacy of alternative crime control strategies. For example, innovative efforts in Hawaii to monitor drug use among probationers with swift yet modest sanctions for violations has greatly reduced drug abuse, absconding from probation officers, and subsequent prison admissions.[4] A growing body of research demonstrates substantial crime-deterrent effects associated with expanding police staffing levels (see Chalfin and McCrary [2013]). There is also ample evidence showing that preventing high-risk youth from dropping out of school substantially lowers the risk of incarceration as an adult (see Lochner and Moretti [2004]).

Diminishing marginal returns and the current low average incapacitation effect of prisons, coupled with the availability of viable alternative crime control tools, strongly suggest that we could substantially scale back our use of incarceration and maintain current, historically low crime rates. Doing so requires that we revisit, reevaluate, and modify the changes in sentencing policies that have occurred since the early 1980s, a process that perhaps has begun with the 2013 policy change that Holder announced. Scaling back our use of incarceration would make a large dent in the reentry challenge because, quite simply, there would be fewer people reentering society from prison.

How would we scale back the use of prison? First, our sentencing philosophy needs to shift in the direction of reserving involuntary confinement for those who pose the greatest risk and alternative sanctions for those who do not. Long mandatory minimum sentences for possession of small amounts of drugs with intent to sell, life terms for third strike offenders convicted of felony larceny (theft with value over what is often a relatively low threshold), and parole revocations triggering new prison terms for technical violations (such as failing a drug test or missing an appointment) all provide examples of sanctions that add to our incarceration rate without preventing much crime. While violations of the law certainly must be met with a sanction, more modest (but perhaps more swift and certain) sanctions would likely achieve similar ends at lower cost.

Sentencing decisions generally are made by the interactions of local district attorneys (often elected officials) and local circuit court judges (sometimes elected, sometimes appointed). In states with very severe sentencing policies, district attorneys tend to wield great power, as the threat of a harsh mandatory minimum sentence will induce many defendants to plead. County employees (district attorneys in particular) also exert great influence over who is sent to prison while state government picks up the tab for subsequent incarceration. This collage of incentives from the perspective of local policymakers certainly tips the scale toward incarceration rather than locally based sanctioned and rehabilitation services. Hence, in addition to revisiting and perhaps undoing many categories of mandatory minimum sentences, creating better incentives for local government to not overuse state prisons would reduce both the prison population and by extension the magnitude of the prisoner reentry challenge. For example, states could share cost-savings with localities that reduce admissions to state prison or introduce taxes for states that appear to overuse the system relative to a determined benchmark.

IMPROVING THE PROCESS OF TRIAGING
THE REENTRY POPULATION

There are several stylized facts that emerge from research on the recidivism of released prison inmates. First, the likelihood of being rearrested drops with time since release, with particularly high risk of rearrest in the weeks immediately following release. Whether this is due to the process of adapting to life outside or the selective rearrest of those most likely to fail on parole is an open question. Nonetheless, from an actuarial point of view, time since release is a strong predictor of the likelihood of future offending.

Second, among those released on any given day, roughly one-third will have no further interaction with the criminal justice system. Roughly two-thirds will be rearrested within three years, and a much smaller fraction will be reconvicted of a new felony offense.

Third, with time it appears to be the case that the offending rate of those released from prison eventually declines to the rate of those who have never been to prison. At present there are only a few research papers that attempt to estimate this threshold. However, the findings to date suggest that within 7 to 10 years, the arrest and conviction rates of prison releases fall to that of the general population (see Blumstein and Nakamura [2009] and Kurlycheck, Bushway, and Brame [2012]).

Assume for the moment that those who do not reoffend for 7 years are fundamentally different from other released offenders in that their likelihood of offending was low from the day they left prison. Criminologists refer to such individuals as immediate desistors. Suppose further that we could identify these individuals immediately. One might reasonably presume that employers would be more willing to give such individuals a chance, smoothing their transition into society, and likely reducing the chance that these low-risk individuals encounter further legal trouble. Moving this third of individuals into more conventional roles earlier would free up resources for service provision for harder-to-serve and high-risk releases.

To be sure, if we rely solely on recidivism outcomes and time since release, we would have to wait 7 to 10 years to identify such individuals. However, what if we could use existing postrelease programs to identify them sooner, improve their chances the first few years out, and provide better information to prospective employers? This very creative line of thinking was recently articulated in a provocative article by criminologists Shawn Bushway and Robert Apel (2012). The authors argue that policymakers should strive to create avenues through which immediate desistors can reveal themselves to corrections officials, parole and probation officers, and employers. Such individuals would be good candidates for early release or greater latitude while in community corrections, and have better chances at procuring employment. Of course, the avenues for providing such a signal must be costly to the inmate, probationer, or prison releasee. If not, everyone would signal that they were an immediate desistor and attempt to reap the benefits associated with the label (and ultimately undermine the credibility of the signal). Alternatively, if acquiring the signal required real effort on the part of the person in question (participation and successful completion of an education program, honest efforts, and successful compliance with the requirements of a transitional jobs program), only those who are truly motivated to leave the life of crime and assume more conventional roles will acquire the signal in question.

In the previous chapter, I devoted considerable attention to discussing impact evaluations of various programs designed to improve the employment prospects of former prisoners and other high-risk individuals with an eye on reducing recidivism. The results from these evaluations are mixed, with some showing promise and others showing disappointingly little impact on future criminal offending. I also noted that nonexperimental studies that compare program participants to nonparticipants generally show large differences in recidivism, with participants faring considerably better. Such differences are also observed within the programs subject to randomized control evaluations. For example, of those participants in New York's CEO program who worked four quarters and were successfully placed in an unsubsidized job, only 10 percent were arrested, convicted, or incarcerated within a year. Among those who did not perform well in the program, 44 percent recidivated. From the standpoint of a program effect evaluator, such a difference might be attributed to unobserved differences in motivation between those who complete the program and those who do not. However, it must certainly be the case that, at a minimum, those who successfully completed the program are revealing that they as a group are disproportionately composed of immediate desistors.

Bushway and Apel (2012) argue that many reentry programs, particularly transitional employment programs, generate substantial value in improving information about individual recidivism risk precisely through the signals that a successful program completion sends. With this in mind, we should harness the value of such service providers as screeners and identifiers of good bets for employers and perhaps for early release from conditional supervision.

One can certainly imagine many arrangements that may allow former inmates to pursue a law-abiding path to self-identify. Completion of a demanding job-training program, substantive educational achievements, demonstrable good behavior while incarcerated, demonstrable efforts and success at victim restitution, and abstaining from drug use may all contribute to achieving such a goal. For employers, the screening role served by labor market intermediaries that also provide reentry programing is particularly valuable and may help employers overcome many of their reservations about hiring former inmates. If signaling and screening by such intermediaries can mitigate stigma for a third of the reentry caseload, this would be an enormous improvement.

Hence, one can envision the establishment of a certification process whereby parole, adult probation, or some authority that monitors the population of released inmates officially certifies compliance and low risk and officially conveys this certification to the community of employers through labor market intermediaries. Such a certification should be based on observed efforts and behavior of released inmates and formally validated through an actuarial analysis of the effect of achieving the compliance certification on actual recidivism outcomes. In essence, the CEO has already done this. Any employer hiring a successful CEO graduate knows that they are hiring someone with a recidivism probability that is one-fourth that of a CEO dropout. In general, we could do more with the information generated in the normal course of providing reentry services to assuage the risk concerns of employers.

SHARING THE RISK WITH EMPLOYERS

Providing an avenue by which low-risk individuals who are committed to a future law-abiding life to self-identify would not only help these individuals but also help employers by identifying low-risk applicants. Given the general reluctance to hire former inmates and the aversion to applicants with a criminal history more generally that I document in Chapter 4, such credible signals may go a long way toward improving the employment prospects of a substantial proportion of former inmates.

This risk-mitigating role points to a more general issue regarding the prisoner reentry challenge. Namely, all agree that employment is central to successful reentry, and most agree that employer concerns regarding potential problems and liability issues associated with hiring former inmates are legitimate. Hence, concrete steps that can be taken to shift some of the risk from employers onto the public sector, and by extension the broader society, may induce more employers to overcome their inhibitions and offer former inmates a chance.

There are extant examples of such efforts. The federal bonding program provides six months of free honesty insurance coverage to employers who hire at-risk job seekers. Expanding this coverage to, say, one year, in conjunction with empirical research showing the large decline in recidivism risk for those who maintain continual employment, may smooth the transition and minimize the costs of subsequently seeking private insurance.

Where would the resources for such programs come from? It could be possible to incorporate the costs of such efforts in any large-scale attempt to redistribute public resources form incarceration to other forms of crime control. For example, the federal Justice Reinvestment Initiative, which aims to help states scale back incarceration and channel the budgetary savings toward other crime control strategies, could be broadened to include a substantial employment component.

Furthermore, creating clear, consistent, and transparent rehabilitation-certification programs would provide former inmates incentives to engage in programming and other efforts likely to hasten criminal desistance, and allow the immediate desistors to self-identify. Combining such programs with tort reforms that limit the liability of employers who hire officially rehabilitated former inmates would further shift the risk burden associated with reentry policy.

To summarize, employment is certainly central to successful reentry for many former inmates, yet employers have legitimate concerns about hiring them. It seems unreasonable to ask employers to bear an undue share of the risk associated with reentry policy, especially as corrections policy choices made over the past few decades are not in any demonstrable way the byproduct of the practices of U.S. employers.

Notes

1. For example, Raphael and Winter-Ebmer (2001) find consistently positive effects of higher unemployment rates on property crime in an analysis of state-level panel data covering roughly the last quarter of the twentieth century. Using similar data, Gould, Weinberg, and Mustard (2002) find that property crime decreases with increasing wages. Grogger (1998) models the decision to participate in crime as a function of the wages one could earn in the labor market using microdata from the 1979 National Longitudinal Survey of Youth (NLSY79) and finds that that higher earnings potential reduces the likelihood of engaging in crime. Freeman (1987) finds that those youth who believe that they could earn more on the streets than in legitimate employment are more likely to engage in criminal activity. Finally, Raphael (2011) simulates where incarcerated offenders would be in the national wage distribution if they were noninstitutionalized and working. This exercise revealed that nearly all would be concentrated in the bottom of the earnings distribution, a fact driven mostly by their low levels of formal education. The absence in the prison population of those with strong earnings potential suggests that low earnings may in part by a driver toward criminal activity.
2. For the full text of the speech, see http://www.justice.gov/iso/opa/ag/speeches/2013/ag-speech-130812.html (accessed August 13, 2013).

3. A third delayed consequence of prisons on crime may operate through the effect of a prison sentence on the future offending of released inmates. This effect can go either way. If prisons rehabilitate then future offending will be below what it otherwise would have been for someone who has served time. Alternatively, the specific experience of prison may deter future crime, as those who have been to prison may not want to go back. In contrast, people adapt to prison culture in a manner that may hamper social skills valued on the outside and increase future criminality. Moreover, inmates are often brutalized, have prolonged exposure to serious offenders, and may also learn how to do time and thus be less deterred by the prospects of a further prison spell. For a thorough review of the long-term effects of serving time in prison see Nagin, Cullen, and Jonson (2009).

4. See the randomized control evaluation of this effort in Hawken and Kleiman (2009).

References

Aizer, Anna, and Joseph J. Doyle Jr. 2013. "Juvenile Incarceration, Human Capital, and Future Crime: Evidence from Randomly Assigned Judges." NBER Working Paper No. 19102. Cambridge, MA: National Bureau of Economic Research.

Apel, Robert, and Gary Sweeten. 2010. "The Impact of Incarceration on Employment during the Transition to Adulthood." *Social Problems* 57(3): 448–479.

Bloom, Howard S., Larry L. Orr, George Cave, Stephen H. Bell, Fred Doolittle, and Winston Lin. 1994. *The National JTPA Study: Overview: Impacts, Benefits, and Costs of Title II-A.* Bethesda, MD: Abt Associates.

Blumstein, Alfred, and Allen J. Beck. 1999. "Population Growth in U.S. Prisons, 1980–1996." *Crime and Justice: A Review of Research* 26: 17–61.

Blumstein, Alfred, and Kiminoro Nakamura. 2009. "Redemption in the Presence of Widespread Criminal Background Checks." *Criminology* 47(2): 327–359.

Bonczar, Thomas P. 2003. *Prevalence of Imprisonment in the U.S. Population, 1974–2001.* Bureau of Justice Statistics Special Report, NCJ 197976. Washington, DC: U.S. Department of Justice. http://www.bjs.gov/content/pub/pdf/piusp01.pdf (accessed September 25, 2013).

Buonanno, Paolo, and Steven Raphael. 2013. "Incarceration and Incapacitation: Evidence from the 2006 Italian Collective Pardon." *American Economic Review* 103(6): 2437–2465.

Bushway, Shawn, and Robert Apel. 2012. "A Signaling Perspective on Employment-Based Reentry Programming: Training Completion as a Desistance Signal." *Criminology and Public Policy* 11(1): 21–50.

Carson, Anne E., and Daniela Golinelli. 2013. *Prisoners in 2012—Advance Counts.* Bureau of Justice Statistics Report, NCJ 242467. Washington, DC: U.S. Department of Justice.

Cave, George, Hans Bos, Fred Doolittle, and Cyril Toussaint. 1993. *JOB-START: Final Report on a Program for School Dropouts.* New York: MDRC. http://www.mdrc.org/sites/default/files/full_416.pdf (accessed September 25, 2013).

Chalfin, Aaron, and Justin McCrary. 2013. "The Effect of Police on Crime: New Evidence from U.S. Cities, 1960 to 2010." NBER Working Paper No. 18815. Cambridge, MA: National Bureau of Economic Research.

Cho, Rosa, and Robert J. Lalonde. 2008. "The Impact of Incarceration in State Prison on the Employment Prospects of Women." *Journal of Quantitative Criminology* 24(3): 243–267.

Drake, Elizabeth K., Steve Aos, and Marna G. Miller. 2009. "Evidence-Based

Public Policy Options to Reduce Crime and Criminal Justice Costs: Implications in Washington State." *Victims and Offenders* 4(2): 170–196.

El v. Southeastern Pennsylvania Transportation Authority 479 F.3d 232 (3d Cir. March 19, 2007).

Equal Employment Opportunity Commission (EEOC). 2012. Equal Employment Opportunity Commission Enforcement Guidance on the Consideration of Arrest and Conviction Records in Employment Decisions under Title VII of the Civil Rights Act of 1964. Washington, DC: EEOC. http://www.eeoc.gov/laws/guidance/arrest_conviction.cfm (accessed September 25, 2013).

Freeman, Richard B. 1987. "The Relationship of Criminal Activity to Black Youth Employment." *Review of Black Political Economy* 16(1-2): 99–107.

General Accounting Office. 1996. *Job Training Partnership Act: Long-Term Earnings and Employment Outcomes.* Report to Congressional Requesters, CAO/HEHS-96-40. Washington, DC: GAO. http://www.gao.gov/assets/230/222393.pdf (accessed September 25, 2013).

Gould, Eric D., Bruce A. Weinberg, and David B. Mustard. 2002. "Crime Rates and Local Labor Market Opportunities in the United States: 1979–1997." *Review of Economics and Statistics* 84(1): 45–61.

Grogger, Jeffrey. 1995. "The Effect of Arrest on the Employment and Earnings of Young Men." *Quarterly Journal of Economics* 110(1): 51–71.

———. 1998. "Market Wages and Youth Crime." *Journal of Labor Economics* 16(4): 756–791.

Hawken, Angela, and Mark Kleiman. 2009. *Managing Drug Involved Probationers with Swift and Certain Sanctions: Evaluating Hawaii's HOPE.* Final report to the National Institute of Justice. Washington, DC: National Criminal Justice Reference Service. https://www.ncjrs.gov/pdffiles1/nij/grants/229023.pdf (accessed September 23, 2013).

Holzer, Harry, Steven Raphael, and Michael Stoll. 2006a. "Perceived Criminality, Criminal Background Checks, and the Racial Hiring Practices of Employers." *Journal of Law and Economics 49(2): 451–480.*

———. 2006b. "How Do Crime and Incarceration Affect the Employment Prospects of Less Educated Black Men?" In *Black Males Left Behind,* Ronald Mincy, ed. Washington, DC: Urban Institute, pp. 67–85.

———. 2007. "The Effect of an Applicant's Criminal History on Employer Hiring Decisions and Screening Practices: Evidence from Los Angeles." In *Barriers to Reentry? The Labor Market for Released Prisoners in Post-Industrial America,* Shawn Bushway, Michael Stoll, and David Weiman, eds. New York: Russell Sage Foundation, pp. 117–150.

Institute for Research on Labor and Employment. 2007. "2007 Survey of California Establishments." Berkeley, CA: University of California, Berkeley, Institute for Research on Labor and Employment.

International Centre for Prison Studies. 2011. World Prison Brief database. London: International Centre for Prison Studies. www.prisonstudies.org/world-prison-brief (accessed January 23, 2014).

Jacobs, Erin. 2012. *Returning to Work after Prison: Final Results from the Transitional Jobs Reentry Demonstration.* New York: MDRC.

Johnson, Rucker, and Steven Raphael. 2012. "How Much Crime Reduction Does the Marginal Prisoner Buy?" *Journal of Law and Economics* 55(2): 275–310.

Jung, Haeil. 2011. "Increase in the Length of Incarceration and the Subsequent Labor Market Outcomes: Evidence from Men Released from Illinois State Prisons." *Journal of Policy Analysis and Management* 30(3): 499–533.

Kessler, Ronald C., Patricia Berglund, Olga Demler, Robert Jin, Kathleen R. Merikangas, and Ellen E. Walters. 2005. "Lifetime Prevalence and Age of Onset Distributions of DSM-IV Disorders in the National Comorobidity Survey Replication." *Archives of General Psychiatry* 62(6): 593–602.

Kessler, Ronald C., Katherine A. McGonagle, Shanyang Zhao, Christopher B. Nelson, Michael Hughes, Suzann Eshleman, Hans-Ulrich Wittchen, and Kenneth S. Kendler. 1994. "Lifetime and 12-Month Prevalence of DSM-III-R Psychiatric Disorders in the United States." *Archives of General Psychiatry* 51(1): 8–19.

Kling, Jeffrey R. 2006. "Incarceration Length, Employment, and Earnings." *American Economic Review* 96(3): 863–876.

Kurlycheck, Megan, Shawn Bushway, and Robert Brame. 2012. "Long-Term Crime Desistance and Recidivism Patterns: Evidence from the Essex County Convicted Felon Study." *Criminology* 50(1): 71–104.

Langan, Patrick A., and David J. Levin. 2002. *Recidivism of Prisoners Released in 1994.* Bureau of Justice Statistics Special Report NCJ 193427. Washington, DC: U.S. Department of Justice. http://www.bjs.gov/content/pub/pdf/rpr94.pdf (accessed September 25, 2013).

Liedka, Raymond, Anne Morrison Piehl, and Bert Useem. 2006. "The Crime Control Effect of Incarceration: Does Scale Matter?" *Criminology and Public Policy* 5(2): 245–275.

Lochner, Lance, and Enrico Moretti. 2004. "The Effect of Education on Criminal Activity: Evidence from Prison Inmates, Arrest, and Self Reports." *American Economic Review* 94(1): 155–189.

Mallar, Charles D., and Craig V. D. Thornton. 1978. "Transitional Aid for Released Prisoners: Evidence from the Life Experiment." *Journal of Human Resources* 13(2): 208–236.

Manpower Development Research Corporation (MDRC). 1980. *Summary Findings of the National Supported Work Demonstration.* Cambridge, MA: Ballinger Publishing Company. http://www.mdrc.org/sites/default/files/full_249.pdf (accessed September 25, 2013).

McConnell, Sheena, and Steven Glazerman. 2001. *National Job Corps Study: The Benefits and Costs of Job Corps*. Report submitted to the Employment and Training Administration, U.S. Department of Labor. Princeton, NJ: Mathematica Policy Research. http://www.mathematica-mpr.com/Publications/PDFs/01-jcbenefit.pdf (accessed September 25, 2013).

Millenky, Megan, Dan Bloom, Sara Muller-Ravett, and Joseph Broadus. 2011. *Staying on Course: Three-Year Results of the National Guard Youth ChalleNGe Evaluation*. New York: MDRC. http://www.mdrc.org/sites/default/files/full_510.pdf (accessed September 25, 2013).

Minton, Todd D. 2013. Jail Inmates at Mid-Year 2012—Statistical Tables. Bureau of Justice Statistics, NCJ 241264. Washington, DC: U.S. Department of Justice. http://www.bjs.gov/content/pub/pdf/jim12st.pdf (accessed September 25, 2013).

Nagin, Daniel S., Francis T. Cullen, and Cheryl Lero Jonson. 2009. "Imprisonment and Reoffending." *Crime and Justice* 38(1): 115–200.

National Archive of Criminal Justice Data. 2003. National Corrections Reporting Program database. Ann Arbor: University of Michigan.

National Research Council. 2007. *Parole Desistance from Crime and Community Integration*. Washington, DC: National Academies Press.

Neal, Derek, and Armin Rick. 2014. "The Prison Boom and the Lack of Black Progress after Smith and Welch." University of Chicago Working Paper. Chicago: University of Chicago.

Owens, Emily. 2009. "More Time, Less Crime? Estimating the Incapacitative Effects of Sentence Enhancements." *Journal of Law and Economics* 52(3): 551–579.

Pager, Devah. 2003. "The Mark of a Criminal Record." *American Journal of Sociology*, 108(5): 937–975.

———. 2007. *Marked: Race, Crime and Finding Work in an Era of Mass Incarceration*. Chicago: University of Chicago Press.

Pager, Devah, and Lincoln Quillian. 2005. "Walking the Talk? What Employers Say vs. What They Do." *American Sociological Review* 70(3): 355–380.

Pager, Devah, Bruce Western, and Bart Bonikowski. 2009. "Discrimination in a Low-Wage Labor Market: A Field Experiment." *American Sociological Review* 74(5): 777–799.

Pettit, Becky, and Christopher Lyons. 2007. "Status and the Stigma of Incarceration: The Labor Market Effects of Incarceration by Race, Class, and Criminal Involvement." In *Barriers to Reentry? The Labor Market for Released Prisoners in Post-Industrial America*, Shawn Bushway, Michael Stoll, and David Weiman, eds. New York: Russell Sage Foundation, pp. 206–226.

Pettit, Becky, and Bruce Western. 2004. "Mass Imprisonment and the Life

Course: Race and Class Inequality in U.S. Incarceration." *American Sociological Review* 69(2): 151–169.

Raphael, Steven. 2006. "The Socioeconomic Status of Black Males: The Increasing Importance of Incarceration." In *Public Policy and the Income Distribution*, Alan Auerbach, David Card, and John Quigley, eds. New York: Russell Sage Foundation, pp. 319–358.

———. 2007. "Early Incarceration Spells and the Transition to Adulthood." In *The Price of Independence: The Economics of Early Adulthood*, Sheldon Danziger and Cecilia Elena Rouse, eds. New York: Russell Sage Foundation, pp. 278–306.

———. 2011. "Improving Employment Prospects for Former Prison Inmates: Challenges and Policy." In *Controlling Crime: Strategies and Tradeoffs*, Phillip J. Cook, Jens Ludwig, and Justin McCrary, eds. Chicago: University of Chicago Press, pp. 521–572.

Raphael, Steven, and Michael A. Stoll. 2013. *Why Are So Many Americans in Prison?* New York: Russell Sage Foundation.

Raphael, Steven, and Rudolf Winter-Ebmer. 2001. "Identifying the Effect of Unemployment on Crime." *Journal of Law and Economics* 44(1): 259–284.

Redcross, Cindy, Megan Millenky, Timothy Rudd, and Valerie Levshin. 2012. *More Than a Job: Final Results from the Evaluation of the Center for Employment Opportunities (CEO) Transitional Jobs Program*. OPRE Report No. 2011-18. New York: MDRC. http://www.mdrc.org/sites/default/files/full_451.pdf (accessed September 25, 2013).

Rossi, Peter, Richard A. Berk, and Kenneth J. Lenihan. 1980. *Money, Work, and Crime: Experimental Evidence*. New York: Academic Press.

Sabol, William J. 2007. "Local Labor-Market Conditions and Post-Prison Employment Experiences of Offenders Released from Ohio State Prisons." In *Barriers to Reentry? The Labor Market for Released Prisoners in Post-Industrial America*, Shawn Bushway, Michael Stoll, and David Weiman, eds. New York: Russell Sage Foundation, pp. 257–303.

Sabol, William J., Katherine Rosich, Kamala Mallik Kane, David Kirk, and Glenn Dubin. 2002. *Influences of Truth-in-Sentencing Reforms on Changes in States' Sentencing Practices and Prison Population*. Report prepared for the National Institute of Justice. Washington, DC. Urban Institute. https://www.ncjrs.gov/pdffiles1/nij/grants/195161.pdf (accessed September 25, 2013).

Schochet, Peter Z., John Burghardt, and Steven Glazerman. 2001. *National Job Corps Study: The Impact of Job Corps on Participants' Employment and Related Outcomes*. Report prepared for the Employment and Training Administration, U.S. Department of Labor. Princeton, NJ: Mathematica Policy Research Inc. http://www.mathematica-mpr.com/publications/PDFs/01-jcimpacts.pdf (accessed September 25, 2013).

Stemen, Don, Andres Rengifo, and James Wilson. 2006. *Of Fragmentation and Ferment: The Impact of State Sentencing Policies on Incarceration Rates, 1975–2002*. Report prepared for the National Institute of Justice. Washington, DC: U.S. Department of Justice. https://www.ncjrs.gov/pdffiles1/nij/grants/213003.pdf (accessed September 25, 2013).

Uggen, Christopher. 2000. "Work as a Turning Point in the Life Course of Criminals: A Duration Model of Age, Employment, and Recidivism." *American Sociological Review* 67(4): 529–546.

U.S. Department of Justice. Bureau of Justice Statistics. 2004. "Survey of Inmates in State and Federal Correctional Facilities." Washington, DC: U.S. Department of Justice.

U.S. Department of Justice. Bureau of Justice Statistics. 2011. *National Prisoner Statistics*. Washington, DC: U.S. Department of Justice. http://www.bjs.gov/index.cfm?ty=dcdetail&iid=269 (accessed January 23, 2014).

U.S. Department of Justice. Office of the Attorney General. 2006. *The Attorney General's Report on the Use of Criminal Background Checks*. Washington, DC: U.S. Department of Justice. http://www.justice.gov/olp/ag_bgchecks_report.pdf (accessed September 25, 2013).

Visher, Christy A., Laura Winterfield, and Mark B. Coggeshall. 2005. "Ex-Offender Employment Programs and Recidivism: A Meta-Analysis." *Journal of Experimental Criminology* 1(3): 295–315.

Vollaard, Ben. 2013. "Preventing Crime through Selective Incapacitation." *Economic Journal* 123(567): 262–284.

Waldfogel, Joel. 1994. "The Effect of Criminal Convictions on Income and the Trust 'Reposed in the Workmen'." *Journal of Human Resources* 29(1): 62–81.

Weaver, Vesla M. 2007. "Frontlash: Race and Development of Punitive Crime Policy." *Studies in American Political Development* 21: 230–265.

Western, Bruce. 2002. "The Impact of Incarceration on Wage Mobility and Inequality." *American Journal of Sociology* 67(4): 526–546.

Wilsou, James Q. 1975. *Thinking about Crime*. New York: Basic Books.

Author

Steven Raphael is Professor of Public Policy at the University of California, Berkeley. His research focuses on the economics of low-wage labor markets, housing, and the economics of crime and corrections. His most recent research focuses on the social consequences of the large increases in U.S. incarceration rates. Raphael also works on the immigration policy, research questions pertaining to various aspects of racial inequality, the economics of labor unions, social insurance policies, homelessness, and low-income housing.

Raphael is the editor in chief of *Industrial Relations* and a research fellow at the University of Michigan National Poverty Center, the University of Chicago Crime Lab, the Public Policy Institute of California, and the Institute for the Study of Labor (IZA) in Bonn, Germany. Raphael holds a PhD in economics from the University of California, Berkeley.

Index

The italic letters *f, n,* or *t* following a page number indicate a figure, note, or table on that page. Double letters mean more than one such item appear on a single page.

Adolescents. *See* Youth (adolescents)
Adults
  incarceration of, 4, 5–6, 5*t,* 7*f,* 8*f,* 9,
    11, 79
  mental illness in general, population,
    37, 41*n*4
  See also Young adults
African Americans, 79
  employment and, 43, 52–53
  male, and discrimination against,
    50–52, 56
  prison inmates as, by gender, 9,
    29–30, 29*t*
  in state or federal prisons, 35, 36*t*
Age
  arrest rates and, 67–68, 72–75
  birth mothers of incarcerated young
    adults and, 29*t,* 30
  prison population and, 35–36, 36*t*
  released prison inmates and, 39, 39*t,*
    60
Aggravated assault, as state prison
    offense, 17*f,* 18, 19, 19*f,* 20, 20*f*
Austria, incarceration rates in, 14, 14*f,*
    24*n*1
Auto theft, 22
  as state prison offense, 17*f,* 19, 19*f,*
    20*f*

Background checks, 56
  data gathering for, 47–52, 57*n*3
  employment and, 3, 11
Behavior
  delinquent, in young adults
    incarcerated or not, 31*t,* 32
  prison inmate, and parole, 21–22
  therapy for (*see* Cognitive behavioral
    therapy)
Belgium, incarceration rates in, 14, 14*f,*
    24*n*1
Birth mothers, age of, 29*t,* 30

BJS (Bureau of Justice Statistics), 5–6, 5*t*
Blacks. *See* African Americans
Bonding insurance, 46, 57*n*1, 88
Burglary, as prison offense, 17*f,* 19, 19*f,*
    20*f,* 36*t*

California, 12*n*1
  employability of former prison
    inmates in, 44–45, 45*f,* 46, 50,
    57*n*2
  San Francisco, and new reentry
    planning model, 76–77
  "three strikes and out" sentencing
    and, 22, 25*n*8
Canada, incarceration rates in, 13–14,
    14*f,* 24*n*1
Center for Employment Opportunities
    (CEO) program
  compared with similar programs,
    69–71, 75–76, 87
  transitional jobs provided by, 68–69,
    86
CEO. *See* Center for Employment
    Opportunities program
ChalleNGe (National Guard Youth
    ChalleNGe) program, 74–75, 76
Child support, as difficult for released
    inmates, 1
Children, 22
  juvenile offenses of, 74, 78*n*6
  likelihood of, being incarcerated
    upon reaching adulthood, 6–7, 7*f,* 8*f*
Cities as study sites. *See under* names of
    states, e.g., Michigan, Detroit
Cocaine, sentencing for, 22
Cognitive behavioral therapy, in-prison,
    64, 76
Corrections reform policy, 79–90
  address the reentry challenge, 79–80,
    89*n*1
  changes in, 12*n*1, 25*n*7

Corrections reform policy, *cont.*
  limit incarceration as punishment,
    81–84, 89n2, 90nn3–4
  sentencing in, 10, 21–23, 25n6
  share risks with employers, 88–89
  triage the reentry population, 80,
    84–87
County jails
  adults incarcerated in, 4, 5–6, 5t, 40
  reentry planning model for, 76–77
Crime, 89n1
  incapacitation of, 2, 12, 82
  sentencing policy changes for, 10,
    21–23, 25n6
  state prison inmates and, 4, 12n1, 17f,
    19f, 20f
  strategies for, control, 80, 83–84
Crime rate, 14, 25n5
  calculation of, 18–19, 24–25n4
  prison affect on, 81–82, 90n3
Crime reduction programs
  employment-based, experimentally
    evaluated, 64–75, 77n4, 78nn5–6
  GED role in, 71, 74
  meta-analysis of, 63–64, 77nn2–3
Criminal history, 38, 41
  author's tabulations of, 29t, 31t
  employability of former prison
    inmates with, 44–47, 45f, 52–56,
    57nn1–2

Delinquent behavior, young adults and,
    31t, 32
Denmark, incarceration rates in, 14, 14f,
    24n1
Discrimination, job-related, 79
  EEOC and, 47, 56
  lawsuits and, 51–52
  subtle forms of, 47–48, 49
Drug Enforcement Administration, 81
Drug treatment programs
  addicts in, as "hard to employ," 66–67
  effectiveness of, 64, 76
Drugs, 25n5
  as federal prison offense, 81
    (*see also* War on Drugs)
  released state prison inmates and,
    offenses, 39t, 40–41

as state prison offense, 4, 17f, 18, 20,
    20f, 21
  See also Cocaine; Substance abuse
Earnings
  effect of pre- and post-prison
    sentence
    on, 53–56, 57n4
  impact of JTPA on, and employment,
    71–71, 78n5
  low, and predictable results, 11, 89n1
Education programs
  in-prison basic, for crime reduction,
    64, 68, 77n3
  remedial, 71, 73, 80
Educational attainment
  high school dropouts, 66, 71, 73–74,
    76
  parents', with young adults
    incarcerated or not, 29t, 30
  released prison inmates and, 39, 39t,
    43, 79, 89n1
  young adults', incarcerated or not,
    30–32, 31t
EEOC. *See* U.S. Equal Employment
    Opportunity Commission
Employers, 57n4
  background checks by, 3, 11, 47–52,
    57n3
  bonding insurance and, 46, 57n1
  immediate desistors and, 85–86
  risk sharing with, 88–89
  wariness of applicants by, 3, 10, 11,
    12, 24, 43–44, 45f
Employment
  audit studies of former inmates and,
    52–53
  challenges that hamper, upon
    mainstream reentry, 2–3, 24,
    44–47
  compensation for, and former
    inmates, 43–44
  crime reduction and, -based
    programs, 64–75, 77n4, 78nn5–6
  implications for former and future
    prison inmates, 75–77
  stable, upon mainstream reentry, 1–2,
    60, 79

Employment, *cont.*
transitional, for groups "hard to
employ," 66–68
Employment outcomes, 73, 76
for former prison inmates, 11–12, 41,
52–56, 57*n*4
European Union, incarceration rates in,
13–14, 14*f,* 24*n*1

Family background
poverty in, 30, 44
young adults' incarcerated or not by,
29*t,* 30
Federal prisons
adults incarcerated in, 4, 5–6, 5*t,* 7*f,*
8*f,* 35–37, 36*t*
drug offenders and, 20–21, 36*t,* 37, 81
Felony offenses, 4, 22
recidivism and, 1, 21, 39*t*
types of, 4, 17*f,* 19*f,* 20*f*
Finland, incarceration rates in, 14, 14*f,*
24*n*1
France, incarceration rates in, 14, 14*f,*
24*n*1

Gate money, as difficult for released
inmates, 1
GED (General Educational
Development), crime reduction
programs and, 71, 74
Gender
adult incarceration by, 5–6, 5*t*
young adults', incarcerated or not by,
29–30, 29*t*
Georgia, Atlanta, and employers'
wariness, 46
Germany, incarceration rates in, 14, 14*f,*
24*n*1
Government regulations, labor market
and, 10
Greece, incarceration rates in, 14, 14*f,*
24*n*1
Hawaii, probationer drug use control in,
83, 90*n*4
Hispanics, 53
prison inmates as, by gender, 5*t,* 6,
7*f,* 8*f,* 29*t*
state or federal prisons, 35, 36*t*

Holder, U.S. Attorney General Eric,
policy shifts and, 81, 83, 89*n*2
Homelessness, 1, 36*t,* 76
Household income, below poverty line,
29*t,* 30, 44
Human capital, investment in, 75–76,
80, 83, 87

Illinois, Chicago, and TJRD in, 69, 70
Immediate desistors, 85–86
Immigration offense, 37
Incapacitation effect, crime reduction
factors and, 2, 12, 82
Incarceration
forces contributing to high U.S., rate,
10, 13–21, 23, 24, 25*n*6, 80
international rates of, 13–15, 14*f,*
24*n*1
scale and scope of U.S., 3–5, 79
U.S. labor market and, 6, 9–12
Income-support programs
LIFE, 65, 75
TARP, 65–66, 75
Information
EEOC guidelines for use of, 11,
50–52
personal, and access to, 47–50, 52
U.S. system of criminal records for,
48–49
Ireland, incarceration rates in, 14, 14*f,*
24*n*1
Italy
evidence against prison as crime
deterrent in, 82–83
incarceration rates in, 14, 14*f,* 24*n*1

Job Corps program, 72–73, 76
Job hiring
former inmates and, 52–56, 57*n*4
legal proscriptions against, 47, 57*n*2
Job placement assistance
prisoner reentry and, 63, 65, 77*n*4
transitional, as prisoner reentry
program, 66–71, 73, 75–76
Job search assistance
traditional workforce development
with, 71
Job skills, 43, 68, 76

Job Training Partnership Act (JTPA),
     out-of-school youth and, 71–72, 76,
     78*n*5
JOBSTART program, 73–74, 76
Justice Reinvestment Initiative, federal,
     88
Juvenile offenses, 74, 78*n*6

Labor markets, 1, 53
     crime reduction and, 79–80, 89*n*1
     incarceration and U.S., 6, 9–12, 24,
          41, 56
     service intermediaries to, 38, 56, 87
Larceny offense, 83
     fraud and, as state prison offenses,
          17*f*, 18, 19, 19*f*, 20, 20*f*
Latinos. *See* Hispanics
Legal proscription, job hiring and, 47
Liability concerns, employers and,
     46–47, 89
LIFE. *See* Living Insurance for Ex-
     Prisoners
Life skills training, 74–75, 76
Living Insurance for Ex-Prisoners
     (LIFE), as income-support
     program for reentry, 65, 75
Luxembourg, incarceration rates in, 14,
     14*f*, 24*n*1

Mandatory minimum sentencing, 22,
     81, 83
Massachusetts, Boston, and employers'
     wariness, 46
Men prison inmates
     adult, by race, 5*t*, 6, 7*f*, 9, 11
     work experience of, 32–33, 34*f*, 79
     young, by race and family
          background, 29–30, 29*t*
Mental illness, 80
     general adult population with, 37,
          41*n*4
     inmate presentation of, 3, 11, 36–37,
          36*t*, 43
Mexico, incarceration rates in, 13–14,
     14*f*, 24*n*1
Michigan, Detroit, employment in, 46,
     69
Minnesota, St. Paul, and TJRD in, 69

Minority races, 56
     audit studies with, and employment
          discrimination, 52–53
     inmate disproportionality and, 3, 11,
          41, 43, 52
Misdemeanor, county jails and, 4
Murder, 22
     as state prison offense, 17*f*, 19*f*, 20,
          20*f*

National Guard Youth ChalleNGe
     program, 76
     life skills training in, 74–75
National Supported Work (NSW)
     intervention, transitional jobs
     provided by, 66–68, 75
Netherlands
     evidence against prison as crime
          deterrent in, 82–83
     incarceration rates in, 14, 14*f*, 24*n*1
New York (State), NYC, and employers'
     wariness in, 46, 53
NSW. *See* National Supported Work
     intervention

Occupational training, 71, 73, 76
On-the-job training, as traditional
     workforce development, 71

Parents, 1, 29*t*, 30
Parole boards, inmate behavior and,
     21–22
Parole violation
     consequences of, 4, 20*f*, 40, 83
     state prison inmates for, 4, 17*f*, 18
Pennsylvania, discrimination lawsuit in,
     51–52
Politics, high U.S. incarceration rate and,
     23, 80
Populations
     disadvantaged, 72–75, 79
     general, and adult mental illness, 37,
          41*n*4
     high-risk, and employment-based
          programs, 64–75
     prison, and age, 35–36, 36*t*
Portugal, incarceration rates in, 14, 14*f*,
     24*n*1

Poverty, 30, 44, 60
Prison inmates, 27–41, 57*n*4
    behavior of, and parole boards,
        21–22
    current, 11, 27, 34–37, 41*n*3, 66–67,
        89*n*1
    by educational attainment, 3, 9, 11,
        35, 36*t*
    former (*see* Prison inmates, released)
    future, 27, 28–34, 54, 76
    by gender or race, 5–9, 5*t*, 7*f*, 8*f*, 35,
        36*t*
    rehabilitation of, 21, 23, 76, 89
        (*see also* Reentry programs)
Prison inmates, released
    criminal histories and bondability of,
        46, 57*n*1
    difficulties faced by, 1, 2–3, 43
    empirical portrait of, 11, 35, 38–41,
        39*t*, 79
    employment implications for, 75–77
    employment outcomes for, 11–12,
        41, 52–56, 57*n*4
    policies for moving toward (*see*
        Corrections reform policy)
    stable employment needed by, 1–2,
        38
    supervision of, 12*n*1, 40, 87
    time served, 39, 39*t*
Probation departments
    coordination of city and county,
        76–77
    local, and supervision of released
        prison inmates, 4, 12*n*1
Property offenses
    released state prison inmates and,
        39*t*, 40–41, 65, 77*n*4
    unemployment and, 80, 89*n*1
    See also Auto theft; Burglary;
        Robbery

Race
    adult incarceration by, 5–6, 5*t*
    young adults incarcerated or not by,
        29–30, 29*t*
    See also Minority races
Rape and sexual assault, as state prison
    offense, 17*f*, 19, 19*f*, 20, 20*f*

Recidivism
    as difficulty for released inmates, 1,
        24
    employment and, 79–80
    rearrest rate of former inmates and,
        59–60, 68–69, 84–85
    reduced, and support programs,
        65–66, 76, 86
    risk of, 21, 52, 87
Reentry, 59, 76
Reentry programs, 77*n*1
    experimental, and results, 64–75,
        77*n*4
    experimental, and their evaluation,
        61–62
    new model for, 76–77
    nonexperimental, 62–64, 76,
        77*nn*2–3, 86
    randomization in evaluation of,
        61–62, 63
    services provided by, 60–61, 77, 80
Risk aversion, employers and, 43–44,
    46–47, 85, 88–89
Robbery
    as prison offense, 17*f*, 19, 19*f*, 20,
        20*f*, 36*t*
    See also Auto theft

Safer Foundation, reentry programs and,
    70
Sentencing policy
    priorities in federal, 81, 83–84, 89*n*2
    U.S. incarceration rate and, 24, 81
    U.S. reforms in, 10, 21–23, 25*n*7
Service providers
    crime reduction programs and, 61,
        77*n*1
    immediate desistors and, 85–86
    labor markets and, 38, 56, 87
    pre- and postrelease, 76–77
    reentry programs and, 60, 61, 69–70,
        80
Social security taxes, inmates and, 57*n*4
Social skills, prison culture and, 90*n*3
Society for Human Resource
    Management, background-check
    data from, 50, 57*n*3

*Southeastern Pennsylvania
Transportation Authority, El v.,*
discrimination and, 51–52
Spain, incarceration rates in, 14, 14*f,*
24*n*1
State parole officers, 4, 12*n*1, 61
State prisons
admission rates to, 16–18, 17*f,* 19*f,*
24*n*3, 24–25*n*4
adults incarcerated in, 4, 5–6, 5*t,* 7*f,*
8*f,* 35–37, 36*t*
crime reduction programs in, 64, 77*n*3
time served in, 16, 19–21, 20*f*
Substance abuse
alternative strategy to control, 83,
90*n*4
inmate history of, 3, 11, 43
jail-based and in-prison treatment
programs for, 64, 80
See also Drug treatment programs
Sweden, incarceration rates in, 14, 14*f,*
24*n*1

TARP. *See* Temporary Aid Research
Project
Temporary Aid Research Project
(TARP), as income-support
program for reentry, 65–66, 75
Therapy, cost-effectiveness of. *See*
Cognitive behavioral therapy
"Three strikes and out" sentencing, 22, 83
Transitional Jobs Reentry Demonstration
(TJRD), compared with similar
programs, 69–71, 75–76
Triple-nons, definition, 12*n*1
"Truth-in-sentencing" law, 22

Unemployment, property crime and, 80,
89*n*1
Unemployment history, applicant, and
employer wariness, 45, 45*f,* 56
Unemployment insurance, 57*n*4, 65
United Kingdom, incarceration rates in,
14, 14*f,* 24*n*1
United States (U.S.), incarceration
statistics in, 5–9, 5*t,* 7*f,* 8*f,* 14*f,*
15*f,* 24*n*2
See also under Labor markets

U.S. Census Bureau, adult incarceration
statistics from, 5*t*
U.S. Department of Justice, 5–6, 5*t*
Attorney General of, 81, 83, 89*n*2
U.S. Equal Employment Opportunity
Commission (EEOC),
discrimination prohibited by, 47,
50–51, 56
U.S. law and legislation
civil rights, 52
job training partnerships, 71–72, 78*n*5
sentencing, 22–23, 80
Urban study sites. *See* cities under names
of states, e.g., Michigan, Detroit

Violent crime
prison inmates and, 4, 17–18, 17*f,* 19,
20*f,* 36*t,* 37
released prison inmates and, offenses,
39*t,* 40–41, 82
Violent Crime Control and Law
Enforcement Act (1994), 22–23
Vocational education, 64, 73, 77*n*3

Wages, crime as function of, 79–80,
89*n*1
War on Drugs, sentencing policy changes
in, 10
Washington State Institute of Public
Policy, rehabilitation review by,
76
Weapons violations
prison inmates and, 4, 36*t*
released prison inmates and,
offenses,
39*t,* 40–41
Welfare recipients, as "hard to employ,"
66–67, 73
Wisconsin, Milwaukee, and employment,
46, 52–53, 69
Women prison inmates
by race, 5*t,* 6, 7–8, 8*f*
work experience of young, compared
to those not incarcerated, 32–33,
33*f*
young, by race and family
background, 29–30, 29*t*
Work experience, 89*n*1

applicants' minimal, and employer
    wariness to hire, 43, 45, 45*f*
  incarcerated or not and, 32–33, 33*f,*
    34*f,* 41, 79
Workforce development, 64
  out-of-school youth and, 71–72, 78*n*5

Young adults, 11
  educational attainment of,
    incarcerated or not, 30–32, 31*t*
  gender and race of, incarcerated or
    not, 29–30, 29*t*
  work experience of, incarcerated or
    not, 32–33, 33*f,* 34*f*
Youth (adolescents), 89*n*1
  disadvantaged, and crime reduction
    programs, 72–75
  as future inmates, 27, 28–34, 83
  gender and race of, incarcerated or
    not by young adulthood, 29–30,
    29*t*
  incarceration of, 28–29, 41*nn*1–2
  JTPA and, 71–72, 78*n*5
  juvenile offenses of, 74, 78*n*6

About the Institute

The W.E. Upjohn Institute for Employment Research is a nonprofit research organization devoted to finding and promoting solutions to employment-related problems at the national, state, and local levels. It is an activity of the W.E. Upjohn Unemployment Trustee Corporation, which was established in 1932 to administer a fund set aside by Dr. W.E. Upjohn, founder of The Upjohn Company, to seek ways to counteract the loss of employment income during economic downturns.

The Institute is funded largely by income from the W.E. Upjohn Unemployment Trust, supplemented by outside grants, contracts, and sales of publications. Activities of the Institute comprise the following elements: 1) a research program conducted by a resident staff of professional social scientists; 2) a competitive grant program, which expands and complements the internal research program by providing financial support to researchers outside the Institute; 3) a publications program, which provides the major vehicle for disseminating the research of staff and grantees, as well as other selected works in the field; and 4) an Employment Management Services division, which manages most of the publicly funded employment and training programs in the local area.

The broad objectives of the Institute's research, grant, and publication programs are to 1) promote scholarship and experimentation on issues of public and private employment and unemployment policy, and 2) make knowledge and scholarship relevant and useful to policymakers in their pursuit of solutions to employment and unemployment problems.

Current areas of concentration for these programs include causes, consequences, and measures to alleviate unemployment; social insurance and income maintenance programs; compensation; workforce quality; work arrangements; family labor issues; labor-management relations; and regional economic development and local labor markets.

CPSIA information can be obtained at www.ICGtesting.com
Printed in the USA
BVOW04s0308230514

354324BV00006B/10/P